"How to hear His Voice"

LISTENING TO
THE VOICE

Martin D. Powell, Ph.D.

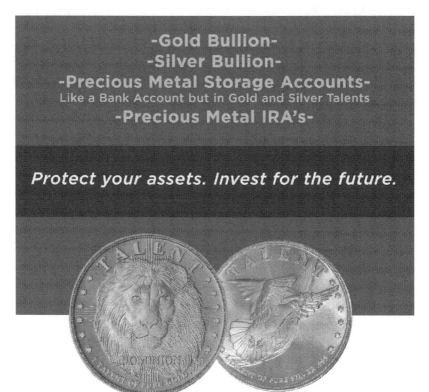

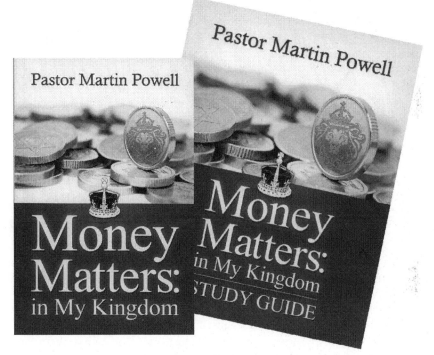

Endorsements

Dr. Martin Powell's latest book, *Listening to the Voice*, is a riveting and well-crafted masterpiece and fascinating narrative that chronicles the plot twists and turns of a life fully surrendered to the lordship of Jesus, across several continents, careers, industries and decades. This powerful saga of learning to hear and obey the voice of God and to partner with the Holy Spirit will have you sitting on the edge of your seat and wanting more.

From a classically trained clarinet soloist for symphonies, to a church pastor to an entrepreneur, to a business owner who designs, mints and markets gold and silver coinage (talents), Martin has repeatedly demonstrated remarkable skill, tenacity, courage and discipline in his journey with God. I recommend both the author and his new book, and unequivocally commend them to you without reservation and with my full endorsement.

Dr. Bruce Cook
Chairman & CEO, KCIA, Kingdom House,
VentureAdvisers.com, Inc.

Martin Powell in *Listening To The Voice* shares from his big, transformed heart the amazing faith journey the Lord has led him on in this inspiring and insightful book full of supernatural discoveries, healings, provision, and victories. Do you want to live life to the fullest? Enjoy the powerful and profound truths found in the living word of the Bible that we can and should hear the 'voice' of our Lord by the Holy Spirit. It's not only possible to hear the voice but essential for us to hear the voice of the Lord for our own life and also for our families, ministry or business. With many scriptural references and practical exercises this book can change your life in short order if you apply the word and inquire of the Lord and listen and obey (shmah). I see spiritual eyes opening and child-like faith growing in your life as you learn about spiritual warfare and seeing what the Lord is ready and wanting to show you. May you experience new dimensions of revelation and spiritual discovery as you hunger for the Holy fire of the Lord revealed in this life changing book.

Jorge Parrott, Ph.D. Missions Director MorningStar/CMM

Listening to the Voice, is a simple but powerful tool for all who want to hear God's voice for themselves. It is for the beginner as well as the veteran disciple. Using amazing personal stories, Martin Powell leads us from beginner steps into the heart of miracles and spiritual warfare. While deeply profound, the book is enjoyably systematic and practical. I recommend this book for all disciples who want to grow in service and intimacy with the Lord Jesus.

Dr. Peter Wyns, Ph.D. President of Christians for Messiah Ministries

For anyone desiring to listen to the voice of God, this is the essential book for you. In a clear, conversational and confessional manner, Martin Powell presents a powerful and Biblically sound teaching on how to receive and develop this spiritual gift in your own life. In this teaching you will come to understand and believe that the Lord wants to speak to you and to speak powerful things into your life and work for the Kingdom. These gifts are essential for every born again believer to successfully serve and to please the Lord in these challenging times.

James Durham, Higher Calling Ministries.

I have known Martin Powell for many years. He is one of those rare individuals who is extremely spiritually gifted, yet has a great sense of humor and an ability to teach in a practical manner. I have gotten to know Martin and his family very well over the years, and he provides not only a great model as a spiritual leader, but also as a husband and father. His knowledge of the scriptures is thorough, and his application is remarkable. He also has an extraordinary blend of practical, faith-based bible teachings on wealth generation that is rare.

Dave Yarnes, Vice President of MorningStar Ministries

Listening to the Voice

Published by:
Kingdom Talents Publishing
375 Star Light Drive
Fort Mill, SC 29715

www.kingdom-talents.com

ISBN 978-1974615933, 1974615936

Printed in the United States of America
First printing. 2017

To correspond with Dr. Martin Powell, please send your letter via email to: Martin@Kingdom-Talents.com You may also contact us in writing at: Dr Martin Powell, 375 StarLight Dr, Fort Mill, SC 29715 USA

We would love to hear from you, and welcome your comments and thoughts about this book. If you desire Martin to come and minister the Word of God and perform his music in your Church, please mention this when you write.

Contents

Chapter 1-The Early Days
pg. 10

Chapter 2-Hearing Voices – Is it Scriptural?
pg.12

Chapter 3-Born Again and Baptisms
pg.22

Chapter 4-How Do I Hear His Voice?
pg. 27

Chapter 5-Finding My Cross
pg.39

Chapter 6-An Arranged Marriage – Talents Music Shop
pg.42

Chapter 7-King David
pg.49

Chapter 8-The Major Prophets and the Voice
pg.57

Chapter 9-New Haven Fellowship
pg. 69

Chapter 10-Elijah versus Elisha
pg. 72

Chapter 11-Having Eyes to See
pg. 78

Chapter 12-Fighting For the Life of My Son David
pg. 83

Chapter 13-Put On the Full Armor of God
pg. 87

Chapter 14-Fighting in the Spirit
pg. 105

Chapter 15-USA and MorningStar
pg. 112

Chapter 16-Part II of My Life – Living in the USA
pg. 116

Chapter 17-Killing Leviathan
pg. 120

Chapter 18-Kingdom Talents
pg. 125

Chapter 19-How to Become One of Jesus' Sheep
pg. 131

Chapter 20-Introduction to Exercises Listening to the Voice
pg. 138

Chapter 21-Conclusion
pg. 162

About the Author
pg.164

This book is dedicated to:

Father

Jesus

Holy Spirit

Chapter 1

The Early Days

My earliest recollection of hearing God's voice was at age four. I know that I was four because I had been told that I was not able to attend the catechism classes as I was too young. One had to be five years old.

Sitting outside of the class listening to the other children discussing the Bible stories, I thought this was unfair as I already knew these stories. It was then that I heard a voice saying "You are going to be a preacher".

I will always be grateful to the Catholic Church and my mother for giving me my faith in Jesus Christ.
Later I would go on to fulfill the Catholic mile stones of 'first communion', 'being an altar boy', and 'confirmation'.

As a teenager I stopped going to church, music and worldly pursuits became my gods.

The Lord continued to try to woo me back though, often through my mother, Marion Louisa Powell. We used to call her 'mum and the God squad' or 'mum and the Bible bashers'.

One day, not unusually, she was trying to get me to read a book, it was by David Wilkerson.
"No, mum." I squirmed, I did not want to know about God. Later that day, I was walking through a field and I said "OK God, if you really want me to read that book, then put it on the pillow of my bed and I will read it." I did not expect Him to do it. As I walked into my bedroom, there was the book lying on my pillow. Without thinking I said "I'm not reading that." Instantly I heard a strong voice inside me, "You said you would!" There was no doubt to who was talking to me, strong and authoritative. I read the book!

I had many opportunities to give my life back to God, I was a prodigal son, yet for some reason I never followed through with it. This came dramatically to a head, whilst I was studying at the Royal Academy of Music in London. My life had become a mixture of success and sadness.

Life was going very well, on the surface, at the Academy. Before I had finished my 3rd year I had won all the prizes available as a soloist. I then went on to win International prizes. I had played to all my heroes, Thea King, Tony Pay, Karl Leister and even had an agent, whilst I was a student. But romantically I was getting through the girls, whenever anything became serious and took time away from my practice, I would break the relationship. I started to feel the inward wounds and wondered about how God put my mum and dad together. My mother had told me their testimony as to how God brought them together.
I started to wish that I had never been in a romantic relationship and wished I could start again.

It was then that I had the most important meeting of my life.

God appeared to me in a dream. I was standing in a church and the room filled with a bright light. Out of the light a voice spoke. "Martin you have had many opportunities to work for me, this is your last chance. Make a decision right now who you will work for, Me or My enemy". I said that I would work for Him. That was the best decision I have ever made and I have never regretted it for an instant.

Chapter 2

Hearing Voices-
Is It Scriptural?

There are many voices to hear, each voice coming from somewhere.

Jesus said 'my sheep will recognize My voice'.

> And when he putteth forth his own sheep, he goeth before them, and the sheep follow him: for **they know his voice**. [5] And a stranger will they not follow, but will flee from him: for they know not the voice of strangers. (John 10:4-5 KJV)

Here Jesus is telling us that his sheep will know his voice, and that there are more voices 'the voice of strangers'.

One of the benefits of being one of His sheep is 'knowing/ recognizing His voice.'

(Most people reading this book will already be a Christian, if you are not then turn to chapter 19 'How to become one of Jesus' sheep'.)

Many psychiatric hospitals are full of people who 'hear voices'. As these institutions are mainly run by the world, and not Christians, most of these unfortunate people are not believers.

Personally I would say that the majority of them are in fact hearing voices. Whether it is the voice of God or the voice of a stranger/demon is the pertinent question.

As there are many voices to hear, we need a method to differentiate what we are hearing.

The primary method for testing a voice is--does the content of the message line up with the written Word of God?

e.g. If I heard a voice saying "Steal the camera".

Well the Bible says 'Thou shalt not steal'.

Therefore the voice that was talking was NOT the Holy Spirit, but some other spirit.

Jesus dealt with the devil in the same way, when the devil was talking to Him.

> Then was Jesus led up of the Spirit into the wilderness to be tempted of the devil. ² And when he had fasted forty days and forty nights, he was afterward an hungred. ³ And when the tempter came to him, he said, If thou be the Son of God, command that these stones be made bread. ⁴ But he answered and said, **It is written, Man shall not live by bread alone, but by every word that proceedeth out of the mouth of God**. ⁵ Then the devil taketh him up into the holy city, and setteth him on a pinnacle of the temple, ⁶ And saith unto him, If thou be the Son of God, cast thyself down: for it is written, He shall give his angels charge concerning thee: and in *their* hands they shall bear thee up, lest at any time thou dash thy foot against a stone. ⁷ Jesus said unto him, **It is written again, Thou shalt not tempt the Lord thy God**. ⁸ Again, the devil taketh him up into an exceeding high mountain, and sheweth

him all the kingdoms of the world, and the glory of them; ⁹ And saith unto him, All these things will I give thee, if thou wilt fall down and worship me. ¹⁰ Then saith Jesus unto him, **Get thee hence, Satan: for it is written, Thou shalt worship the Lord thy God, and him only shalt thou serve.** ¹¹ Then the devil leaveth him, and, behold, angels came and ministered unto him. (Matthew 4:1-11 KJV)

Notice how the devil was trying to be cunning with Jesus. He wasn't asking Jesus to do things that were obviously wrong like 'murdering someone', but he was even using the written word of God in the way he spoke to Him.

'For it is written, He shall give his angels charge concerning thee: and in *their* hands they shall bear thee up, lest at any time thou dash thy foot against a stone.'

Jesus was ready to be tested as he knew the Word of God and was able to recognize who was talking to Him and be able to say 'Get thee hence, Satan'.

So as the primary method of testing the words that we hear, are the written words of God, we will be using the Holy Scriptures to test all that we will be studying.

> Study to shew thyself approved unto God, a workman that needeth not to be ashamed, rightly dividing the word of truth. (2 Timothy 2:15)

Let us examine whether hearing voices is scriptural.

Did Adam hear God speak?

> And they heard the voice of the LORD God walking in the garden in the cool of the day: and Adam and his wife hid themselves from the presence of the LORD

14

God amongst the trees of the garden. (Genesis 3:8)

Yes, Adam heard God speak.
But that may have been because God was appearing to him in bodily form.

Did Noah hear God speak?

> And God said unto Noah, The end of all flesh is come before me; for the earth is filled with violence through them; and, behold, I will destroy them with the earth. (Genesis 6:13)

Yes, Noah heard God speak.
It does not tell us in what form God spoke to Noah.

Did Abraham hear God speak?

> And it came to pass after these things, that God did tempt Abraham, and **said unto him**, Abraham: and he said, Behold, here I am. ² And he said, Take now thy son, thine only son Isaac, whom thou lovest, and get thee into the land of Moriah; and offer him there for a burnt offering upon one of the mountains which I will tell thee of. (Genesis 22:1-2)

Yes, Abraham heard God speak to him. He also heard the voice of an angel talking to him from heaven.

> And **the angel of the LORD** called unto Abraham **out of heaven** the second time, ¹⁶ And said, By myself have I sworn, saith the LORD, for because thou hast done this thing, and hast not withheld thy son, thine only son: ¹⁷ That in blessing I will bless thee, and in multiplying I will multiply thy seed as the stars of the heaven, and as the sand which is upon the sea shore; and thy seed shall possess the gate of his enemies; ¹⁸ And in thy seed shall all the nations of the earth be blessed; **because thou hast obeyed my voice.** (Genesis 22:15-18)

Did Samuel hear God speak?

> And ere the lamp of God went out in the temple of the LORD, where the ark of God was, and Samuel was laid down to sleep; ⁴ That the LORD called Samuel: and he answered, Here am I. ⁵ And he ran unto Eli, and said, Here am I; for thou calledst me. And he said, I called not; lie down again. And he went and lay down. ⁶ And the LORD called yet again, Samuel. And Samuel arose and went to Eli, and said, Here am I; for thou didst call me. And he answered, I called not, my son; lie down again. ⁷ Now Samuel did not yet know the LORD, neither was the word of the LORD yet revealed unto him. ⁸ And the LORD called Samuel again the third time. And he arose and went to Eli, and said, Here am I; for thou didst call me. And Eli perceived that the LORD had called the child. ⁹ Therefore Eli said unto Samuel, Go, lie down: and it shall be, if he call thee, that thou shalt say, Speak, LORD; for thy servant heareth. So Samuel went and lay down in his place. ¹⁰ And the LORD came, and stood, and called as at other times, Samuel, Samuel. Then Samuel answered, **Speak; for thy servant heareth.** ¹¹ And the LORD said to Samuel, Behold, I will do a thing in Israel, at which both the ears of every one that heareth it shall tingle..................(1 Samuel 3:3-11)

Yes, Samuel heard God speak. As we can see there was no form to go with the voice. In fact he thought it must have been Eli speaking to him. Eli helped him to respond to the voice with— Speak Lord; for thy servant heareth.

This is the cry of all that truly want to hear the voice of the Master. If Jesus is not your Lord then it is unlikely you will hear Him.

The reason this book it titled 'Listening to the Voice', and not 'Hearing the Voice' can be found in the Hebrew word שָׁמַע shama.

According to Strong's dictionary this word has the meaning:
1) to hear, listen to, obey.

To simply hear God's voice is not enough. We need to be attentive, to listen to it, ready to obey.

When we hear God's voice and don't obey it we start to become 'dull of hearing'.

> For this people's heart is waxed gross, and their ears are dull of hearing, and their eyes they have closed; lest at any time they should see with their eyes, and hear with their ears, and should understand with their heart, and should be converted, and I should heal them. [16] But blessed are your eyes, for they see: and your ears, for they hear. (Matthew 13:15-16)

> Of whom we have many things to say, and hard to be uttered, seeing **ye are dull of hearing.** [12] For when for the time ye ought to be teachers, ye have need that one teach you again which be the first principles of the oracles of God; and are become such as have need of milk, and not of strong meat. [13] For every one that useth milk is unskilful in the word of righteousness: for he is a babe. [14] But strong meat belongeth to them that are of full age, even those **who by reason of use** have their **senses exercised** to discern both good and evil. (Hebrews 5:11-14)

> But be ye **doers of the word, and not hearers only,** deceiving your own selves. (James 1:22)

After a tiring day at work I was travelling home. Sitting on a train on the London Underground, exhausted, I was looking forward to seeing my wife, and having my dinner.

A voice cut across my thoughts.

"Martin, I want you to do something for Me. But I am not going to tell you what it is until you tell me that you will do it."

The Lord was being gracious with me. If He gave me an instruction and I didn't do it, then I would become dull of hearing. Therefore I could make a decision without affecting my hearing.

Also it seemed to me like a test. I was tired, and I wanted to go home. What would He say to me to do? My mind raced to all the possibilities. Starting with the extremes of 'go to Heathrow airport and fly to Africa'!! etc..

I decided to get off the train and sit on a bench to think about it.

I have had to make some hard decisions in my life, but deep down I really, truly, want to please God and obey Him. Sometimes fear will try and stop us obeying Him. But each time I have decided to listen and obey something good has come.

It took me about five minutes of deliberation before I came to the only answer you can give a Lord. Yes - Jesus what do you want me to do? I will commit to doing it without knowing what it is.

He told me to get on the next train. After two stops He told me to get off the train. Then he told me to walk down a corridor. Then He told me to go left. He walked me right into a man that was praying that God would send someone to him.
After meeting the man, I went home. But it seemed as though I 'floated' home. The Lord had given me His joy.

His lord said unto him, Well done, thou good and faithful servant: thou hast been faithful over a few things, I will make thee ruler over many things: enter thou into the joy of thy lord. (Matthew 25:21)

18

Let us revisit what Eli said to Samuel in the NIV version.

So Eli told Samuel,

> "Go and lie down, and if he calls you, say,
>
> **'Speak, LORD, for your servant is listening.'** (1 Samuel 3:9 NIV)

We could carry on with a whole list of people who heard God speak in the Old Testament, that we have not mentioned so far -- David, Solomon, Isaiah, Jeremiah, Ezekiel, Daniel etc.

Did they also hear God speak in the New Testament?

Did Jesus hear God's voice?

> While he yet spake, behold, a bright cloud overshadowed them: and **behold a voice out of the cloud**, which said, This is my beloved Son, in whom I am well pleased; hear ye him. ⁶ And when the disciples heard *it*, they fell on their face, and were sore afraid. (Matthew 17:5-6)

> Father, glorify thy name. **Then came there a voice from heaven**, *saying*, I have both glorified *it*, and will glorify *it* again. ²⁹ The people therefore, that stood by, and heard *it*, said that it thundered: others said, An angel spake to him. ³⁰ Jesus answered and said, This voice came not because of me, but for your sakes. (John 12:28-30)

This voice was so loud that people heard it, but did not necessarily understand it, some even thought it had thundered.

Did Saul, later named the Apostle Paul, hear God speak?

> And as he journeyed, he came near Damascus: and suddenly there shined round about him a light from heaven: [4] And he fell to the earth, and **heard a voice saying unto him**, Saul, Saul, why persecutest thou me? [5] And he said, Who art thou, Lord? And the Lord said, **I am Jesus** whom thou persecutest: *it is* hard for thee to kick against the pricks. [6] And he trembling and astonished said, Lord, what wilt thou have me to do? And the Lord *said* unto him, Arise, and go into the city, and it shall be told thee what thou must do. [7] And the men which journeyed with him stood speechless, hearing a voice, but seeing no man. (Acts 9:3-7)

> And one Ananias, a devout man according to the law, having a good report of all the Jews which dwelt *there*, [13] Came unto me, and stood, and said unto me, Brother Saul, receive thy sight. And the same hour I looked up upon him. [14] And he said, The God of our fathers hath chosen thee, that thou shouldest know his will, and see that Just One, **and shouldest hear the voice of his mouth.** (Acts 22:12-14)

Did the Apostle Peter, hear God speak?

> And (Peter) saw heaven opened, and a certain vessel descending unto him, as it had been a great sheet knit at the four corners, and let down to the earth: [12] Wherein were all manner of fourfooted beasts of the earth, and wild beasts, and creeping things, and fowls of the air. [13] And **there came a voice to him**, Rise, Peter; kill, and eat. [14] But Peter said, Not so, Lord; for I have never eaten any thing that is common or unclean. [15] And **the voice *spake* unto him again the second time**, What God hath cleansed, *that* call not thou common. (Acts 10:11-15)

20

Did the Apostle John, hear God speak?

> I John, who also am your brother, and companion in tribulation, and in the kingdom and patience of Jesus Christ, was in the isle that is called Patmos, for the word of God, and for the testimony of Jesus Christ. [10] I was in the Spirit on the Lord's day, **and heard behind me a great voice**, as of a trumpet, [11] Saying, **I am Alpha and Omega**, the first and the last: and, What thou seest, write in a book, and send *it* unto the seven churches which are in Asia; unto Ephesus, and unto Smyrna, and unto Pergamos, and unto Thyatira, and unto Sardis, and unto Philadelphia, and unto Laodicea. (Revelation 1:9-11)

Chapter 3

Born Again and Baptisms

T he affect of the decision in my dream to work for God did not manifest until a week later. First of all, a friend of mine caught my eye, and did a double take. It was as if she had seen a change in my spirit. She was a member of the Christian Union at the Royal Academy of Music.
It transpired that they had all been praying for me to become a Christian. Thank you.

The Christian Union had invited a preacher, David Cassidy, from the ministry Maranatha, to come and preach at the Academy. A man called Sean Blackman asked me whether I was going to attend the meeting. Before I could say 'no', 'yes' popped out of my mouth. I was astonished before I could correct my mistake Sean had gone. There was nothing I could do about it, I was being caught by my integrity. My mother had always taught me to do what I said.

Reluctantly I attended the meeting and was extremely impressed with what I heard. The preacher, David Cassidy, was talking about the Bible as if he believed it. After attending a second meeting my hand went straight up, when asked who would like to give their lives to Jesus. I was a prodigal son returning home.

I will be forever grateful to the ministry Maranatha led by Bob Weiner. Their work on the mission field meant that I would now be going to heaven and not hell.

At first my mother had mixed feelings. Pleased that I was enthusiastic about working for God, but unsure about this American ministry I was attending, that wasn't the Catholic Church.

Her mind was put to rest though, when at a prayer meeting with her charismatic Catholic friends, the Lord said that she was not to be worried as 'Martin had answered His call and was working for Him now'. Of course there is only one church (body).

> *There is* one body, and one Spirit, even as ye are called in one hope of your calling; ⁵ One Lord, one faith, one baptism. (Ephesians 4:4-5)

We just meet in different buildings, and different organizations. Every sincere believer, who confesses that Jesus is their Lord is part of that body.

About a couple of weeks later I was baptized in the bathroom of a Victorian house in Earls Court London. I was expecting the heavens to open, as I came out of the water, but all I felt was 'wet'.

I was then prayed for, with the laying on of hands, to receive the gift of the Holy Spirit. (See Acts 2:38)

After a little while I was praying in a strange, new language. That was an interesting evening, with the extra complication of being baptized with my arm in plaster. I had been in a motorbike accident two days previously. My right wrist had been broken with a chip out of the bone on my right thumb. The doctors had said that I would not play the clarinet for three months.

On the way home, I was pondering how I had not felt anything spiritual happen during the baptism in water. I was sitting on a London underground train travelling home.

"Martin, give your Bible to the lady sitting opposite you". A voice had suddenly spoken to me.

I stood up and gave her my Bible, saying "God has asked me to give you my Bible". She started reading where I had been reading, I had given her the Bible open where I was studying, and then started to cry.

Was I now to lead my first person to Christ since being baptized?

"Martin, get off the train".   This was rather inconvenient as it was around 11.45pm, and I wanted to go home. As I hesitated the doors started to close. "See, I can't get off now Lord" I replied. As I spoke the doors bounced back open, I had no choice but to get off.

I was at Baker Street tube station, wanting to get home to Wembley. It was late and I wasn't sure when the next train would arrive. I decided to go up the escalators to see if there were any trains due on the Metropolitan line. There was a train waiting, so I jumped onto it. This was great because this line was a faster one then the one I was on. I would get home earlier, because I had listened/obeyed the 'Voice'. What was next?

Sitting down on the train, I decided to try the 'tongues' again. So putting my hand over my mouth, so as not to attract attention, I started praying in this new language again. The words were coming out at breakneck speed, like an old modem. The words were bursting forth as if they had been pent up.

"Are you praying in tongues?", said the lady sitting opposite me. This was a surprise, I didn't realize anyone could hear me, and how could God have arranged for this lady to be sitting opposite me?

"Would you like me to teach you about it, I'm a Bible teacher?" "Yes", I responded to the lady who went on to take me through the Bible expounding on the gift of tongues.

Arriving at my station 'Wembley Park', I decided that I would try praying for something.
"Dear Lord, would you provide me with a bus to take me home." I asked.
As I was walking towards the bus stop, I decided that even though it was very late, almost 1am, I would walk home, so that I could talk to the Lord.

"Dear Lord, I've changed my mind, I think I will walk home, but could you please still send the bus, so that I know you answer prayer." As I reached the bus stop a bus pulled up and the driver asked me if I wanted a ride. I waved him on, and carried on walking. Hmmmm this has been an interesting evening I mused.

"Martin, I would like you to take the plaster cast off your arm." Woah, that is an incredible request, I thought.

My goodness, if that is not God speaking I could wreck my whole playing career. I was a soloist on the clarinet.

This was the first truly difficult thing God had asked me to do. I was a virtuoso clarinetist playing pieces of music at speeds up to 16 notes per second. If my wrist did not heal perfectly, what would happen to my playing?

This was not an easy request.

As it was a 20 minute walk to my home, I had time to think about it.

Eventually I came up with an answer. There were 4 different possibilities.

1. I could not take the plaster off, and the Voice was not God. The result would be that I would be okay.

2. I could not take the plaster off, and the Voice was God. The result would be that I would have let God down on the first hard thing He asked me to do.

3. I could take the plaster off, and the Voice was God. The result would be that He would heal me, and that He would be able to ask me to do harder things.

4. I could take the plaster off, and the voice was not God. Hmmmm well God is big enough to sort this out. After all I had recently given my life to Him, I now believed that God Almighty was real and alive and that I was now working for Him.

When I arrived home, I put my plaster cast under the hot water to soften it. I then managed to tear it off. It was the first time that I had been able to sleep without pain and I was playing my clarinet within a week, not three months. On going back to the hospital for my booked appointment, the new doctor had not realized that I had been in a plaster cast, and the original X-rays now showed NO breaks.

I love working for God.

Chapter 4

How Do I Hear His Voice?

It is impossible to be a Christian without hearing His Voice. Or I can rephrase this to 'It is impossible to be a Christian without having heard His Voice.'

We can perceive this statement from scripture.

> So then faith comes by hearing, and hearing by the word of God. (Romans 10:17)

The way we receive our faith in Christ, that He was raised from the dead and that He, the Christ, is the Son of the living God, is through 'hearing'.

Jesus revealed this truth in this way:

> When Jesus came into the region of Caesarea Philippi, He asked His disciples, saying, "Who do men say that I, the Son of Man, am?" ¹⁴ So they said, "Some say John the Baptist, some Elijah, and others Jeremiah or one of the prophets." ¹⁵ He said to them, **"But who do you say that I am?"** ¹⁶ Simon Peter

> answered and said, **"You are the Christ, the Son of the living God."** [17] Jesus answered and said to him, "Blessed are you, Simon Bar-Jonah, for flesh and blood has not revealed this to you, **but My Father who is in heaven.** (Matthew 16:13-17 NKJV)

There is not one of us, who believes that Jesus is the Son of God, that receives this revelation through flesh and blood.

Belief doesn't come to us simply because someone, flesh and blood, tells us it is true. We have to gain that revelation, not from Earth, but from Heaven. We receive the revelation through our spiritual sense of 'hearing'. We hear from Heaven, faith comes by hearing, and hearing by the word of God.

The starting point for listening to God, is to realize that, as a Christian, we can hear God.

We may have become dull of hearing, but we certainly have heard from Heaven that Jesus is the Christ or we wouldn't be Christians.

Paul wanted to explain how Jesus was a High Priest according to the order of Melchizedek.
But he was finding it hard to explain, as they had become 'dull of hearing'.

> And having been perfected, He became the author of eternal salvation to all who obey Him, [10] called by God as High Priest "according to the order of Melchizedek," [11] of whom we have much to say, and hard to explain, since **you have become dull of hearing.** [12] For **though by this time you ought to be teachers,** you need someone to teach you again the first principles of the oracles of God; and you have come to need milk and not solid food. [13] For everyone who partakes only of milk is unskilled in the word of righteousness, for he is a babe. [14] But solid food belongs to those who are of full age, that is, those who by reason of use have their senses exercised to discern both good and evil. (Hebrews 5:9 - 14 NKJV)

Paul proceeds to say that 'by this time you ought to be teachers'. They had started hearing God, but had become dull of hearing. The time that had lapsed was enough for them to have become teachers but still they were not hearing clearly, in fact, they needed to go back to milk and not solid food.

Paul says that we have 'senses', and that the 'senses' are exercised by using them.

Jesus talks about our ability to use the spiritual senses of hearing and seeing.

"He who has ears to hear, let him hear!" Matthew 11:15 NKJV
"He who has ears to hear, let him hear!" Matthew 13:9 NKJV
"He who has ears to hear, let him hear!" Matthew 13:43 NKJV
"He who has ears to hear, let him hear!" Mark 4:9 NKJV
"If anyone has ears to hear, let him hear." Mark 4:23 NKJV
"If anyone has ears to hear, let him hear!" Mark 7:16 NKJV
"He who has ears to hear, let him hear!" Luke 8:8 NKJV
"He who has ears to hear, let him hear!" Luke 14:35 NKJV

> For the hearts of this people have grown dull. Their ears are hard of hearing, And their eyes they have closed, Lest they should see with their eyes and hear with their ears, Lest they should understand with their hearts and turn, So that I should heal them.' [16] "But blessed are your eyes for they see, and your ears for they hear; (Matthew 13:15-16)

> "But blessed are your eyes for they see, and your ears for they hear; (Matthew 13:16)
> "Having eyes, do you not see? And having ears, do you not hear? (Mark 8:18)

He who has ears to hear, let him hear!!!!!!!

We often talk about how a spiritual point is emphasized through repetition.

> E.g. O earth, earth, earth, Hear the word of the LORD! (Jer 22:29)

Notice how often Jesus has said the same words "He who has ears to hear, let him hear.", this must be very important. In fact I do not know of any other scripture that is repeated so many times.

This may be a good time to pray.

Dear Father in Heaven, I thank you that you gave me faith by hearing, so that I could be saved. By now I should be a teacher. I do not want to be dull of hearing, but would like to have clarity of hearing. A servant needs to hear their Master, please forgive me for not listening attentively and open my ears that I may serve You. Let me have ears to hear. I ask this in the name of Jesus. Amen.

God may talk to us with an audible voice, that is, we are hearing with our physical ears.
But from my own experience, and many others, He mostly talks to us with a spiritual voice, which we hear with our spiritual ears.

The sound of spiritual words, are heard like thoughts in our heart.

> And he said unto them, Why are ye troubled? and why do thoughts arise in your hearts? (Luke 24:38)

In scripture thoughts are always attributed as coming from the heart, not the brain, or the mind.

With our spiritual ears we hear words spoken by spirits.

This is why Paul was careful to convey to us that our spiritual senses could hear/see evil as well as good.

> .. those who by reason of use have their senses exercised to discern both good and evil. (Heb 5:16 NKJV)

As there are many voices to hear, we need to exercise our senses, by using them, to discern whether what we are hearing is good or evil.

The good spirits we can hear are; our own spirit, God the Father, Jesus, the Holy Spirit, and Angels.

> Judas saith unto him, not Iscariot, Lord, how is it that thou wilt manifest thyself unto us, and not unto the world? [23] Jesus answered and said unto him, If a man love me, he will keep my words: and my Father will love him, and we will come unto him, and make our abode with him. (John 14:22-23)

> And the angel said unto me, Wherefore didst thou marvel? I will tell thee the mystery of the woman, and of the beast that carrieth her, which hath the seven heads and ten horns. (Revelation 17:7)

The evil spirits we can hear are: the devil, demons, unclean spirits etc.

> For from within, out of the heart of men, proceed evil thoughts, adulteries, fornications, murders, [22] Thefts, covetousness, wickedness, deceit, lasciviousness, an evil eye, blasphemy, pride, foolishness: [23] All these evil things come from within, and defile the man.. (Mark 7:21-23)

The voice we hear the most internally is our own voice, the voice of our own spirit.

As an exercise, talk to yourself internally. Count numbers one to ten. Can you hear yourself?

Talk louder, softer, slower, faster, kindly, aggressively. This is your spirit. These are not uncontrolled thoughts or pictures, but distinct sounds you are creating in the spirit. Do you recognize your own voice?

Once we recognize our own voice, we can start to recognize other voices.

> And when he putteth forth his own sheep, he goeth before them, and the sheep follow him: for they know his voice. [5] And a stranger will they not follow,

but will flee from him: for they know not the voice of strangers. (John 10:4-5)

Are you ready to start recording God's voice? If so, get yourself a pen and paper, or preferably a journal.

We are going to start a journey that will last for eternity.

I keep a journal on my computer, it is a file called 'Daniel Plan'. Daniel's love for intimacy with God was such that it meant more to him than his own life. He was willing to die, rather than to curtail his time spent with Father. When a law was passed that anyone who petitions any god or man for thirty days, except King Darius would be cast into the den of lions, Daniel continued his regular prayer times. This can be found in the book of Daniel chapter six.

In my journal I type my prayers, and listen to God's responses.

Ok, I hope you are all prepared with pens, paper, computers etc..

Let's ask God to say something to us.

A prayer like the following is suitable.

'Dear Father in Heaven, you said that man shall not live by bread alone, but by every word that proceeds from the mouth of God. I cannot live solely on physical food, what would you like to say to me today? Speak Lord for your servant is listening.'

Now write down what He says.
Remember if you ask for a fish he will not give you a scorpion.

> "If a son asks for bread from any father among you, will he give him a stone? Or if he asks for a fish, will he give him a serpent instead of a fish? 12 "Or if he asks for an egg, will he offer him a scorpion? 13 "If you then, being evil, know how to give good gifts to your children, how much more will your heavenly Father give the Holy Spirit to those who ask Him!"(Luke 11:11-13 NKJV)

We should have one of the following results now:

1   You have heard nothing.
2   You have written down words that you have heard.
3   You have heard something but have not written it down
     because you don't believe it is God.

If you have heard nothing then listen again. When the Lord was teaching me to see in the spirit, He had me looking for over an hour before I saw anything.

Remember what Paul said--

> **..those who by reason of use** have **their senses exercised...** (Heb 5:14)

As a classical musician, I would practice 6 hours a day for many years, to produce a beautiful sound.

Do you want to hear God? Do not give up, keep practicing. It is those who by reason of use, who have their senses exercised. Determine that you will succeed set aside a regular time, like Daniel, to listen.

If you did not hear anything when listening, one of the reasons may be that you have become dull of hearing. This can occur when God had previously spoken to us and we did not do what He said. We can unblock our ears by repenting.

If that is the case pray with me the following:
Dear Father, I am sorry that I did not do the things you asked me to do, (enter your own words here, describing what had been previously asked of you). I know that you are a Holy God and that I need to respect the words you have already said to me. Please forgive me, You are a gracious and merciful God. Wash me clean and open my ears. I will listen and obey your Voice. I ask for this in the name of Jesus.

Please note, that we do not need to obey the voice of strangers, and that we need to test what we hear. But if we 'know' that it was God who spoke to us and we did not obey, then we must repent.

Using the method above I have taught many people to listen to God. My wife Janet, frequently gives me words from the Lord, my mother Marion gives me a weekly word from the Lord, and my Son David, ten years old, daily gives me words from the Lord.

Interestingly my son David gave his first word of prophecy before he was approximately 22 months old.
I was praying in the spirit with my wife Janet in the car, when a small voice came from the car seat in the back. 'Daddy the curse is broken now'. I distinctly remember that he was not yet two years of age.

He would also give me words from the Lord when he didn't even know the meaning of the vocabulary that was being used. He would then ask me what the words meant.

We need to enter the Kingdom of Heaven as a child.

> "Assuredly, I say to you, whoever does not receive the kingdom of God as a little child will by no means enter it."(Mark 10:15)

Whilst listening if you heard something but didn't write it down because you thought it was not God. My advice is to write it down anyway. The purpose of the exercise is to listen. Remember again what Paul said--

> **..those who by reason of use** have **their senses exercised** to discern both good and evil. (Heb 5:14)

When you hear a word, and you think that it is not good then you have discerned that the voice you heard was not God. This is valuable. It is those who through reason of use learn to discern both good and evil. We must keep practicing.

Whilst listening if you have written something down the next step is to test what you have heard.

How to test a word whether it is from God or not.

> Beloved, do not believe every spirit, but test the spirits, whether they are of God; because many false prophets have gone out into the world. (1 John 4:1 NKJV)

When we read this verse it is very easy to think that we need to test all the prophets in the Church that we should make sure that we are not listening to false prophets.

This has to be tempered with the following verses:

> Do not quench the Spirit. [20] Do not despise prophecies. [21] Test all things; hold fast what is good. (1 Thessalonians 5:19-21)

> Beloved, believe not every spirit, but try the spirits whether they are of God: because many false prophets are gone out into the world. (1 John 4:1)

When I read 1 John 4:1 I am normally thinking, 'Help God, I don't want to be the false prophet!'

We shouldn't despise prophecy and we don't want to be the false prophets.

But we are not alone.

The first test, is, as previously mentioned, does the word received line up with the written word of God?

This is quite straightforward, as long as we know the word of God, which is another good reason to study the Bible.

Many messages, are not straightforward, they are neither dismissed or confirmed by the written word.

They may be part right, and part wrong.

The answer can be found in 1 Corinthians.

> Let two or three prophets speak, **and let the others judge.** [30] But if anything is revealed to another who sits by, let the first keep silent. [31] For you can all prophesy one by one, that all may learn and all may be encouraged. [32] And the spirits of the prophets are subject to the prophets. [33] For God is not the author of confusion but of peace, as in all the churches of the saints. (1 Corinthians 14:29-33 NKJV)

We are not alone--the answer is to submit what we are hearing to our Christian brothers and sisters. They may be able to judge the words for us.

Let every word be established by two or three witnesses.
This is a good principle, but it is not always correctly applied.

I have often asked God to confirm a word that I have been given and He has been gracious enough to do it.

I received a letter from my local council in London, they said they were going to compulsorily buy my building, as they were going to widen the main South circular road.

I asked God what to do about it. His response was "Extend the premises".
It was a strange response, so I asked Him again what I should do. "Extend the premises".
Asking for more detail I asked what it was for, and He said that it was to be a recording studio.
I asked for a confirmation, and the next morning I received a telephone call from the wife of a Pastor I knew. "Martin, I have been hearing your name and 'recording studio' all morning. Does it mean anything to you?"

As you can guess, the Council later changed their minds, and many years later a recording studio was built.

That was a quick confirmation to the word I received, but He does not always confirm words.

I think that our motive in wanting a word confirmed is important. Is it because of lack of faith or do we believe, but don't want to do it? God will grow our faith if we ask Him to, remember Sarah and Abraham, how their faith grew so that they could receive the promise of Isaac. Sarah started out laughing.

Also we have to remember that when we die we stand alone before God. Will He say 'well done good and faithful servant'. Or will He say 'you dodged the work set for you to do'.

Have faith, know what the will of the Lord is, pray for it. Eph 5:17, Eph 1:17-23
Remember how Agabus inadvertently was trying to discourage Paul from fulfilling his destiny.

> And as we stayed many days, a certain prophet named Agabus came down from Judea. [11] When he had come to us, he took Paul's belt, bound his own hands and feet, and said, "Thus says the Holy Spirit, 'So shall the Jews at Jerusalem bind the man who owns this belt, and deliver him into the hands of the Gentiles.' " [12] Now when we heard these things, both we and those from that place pleaded with him not to go up to Jerusalem. [13] Then Paul answered, "What do you mean by weeping and breaking my heart? For I am ready not only to be bound, but also to die at Jerusalem for the name of the Lord Jesus." [14] So when he would not be persuaded, we ceased, saying, "The will of the Lord be done."(Acts 21:10-14)

The fact that Paul was going to be bound, did not discourage him from going to Jerusalem, as he was fully convinced in his mind what the Lord had called him to do.

I have always felt that Paul was encouraged and strengthened from the scriptures about the man of God in 1 Kings chapter 13. This man of God was given instructions from God to speak to the altar at Bethel, then he was to return to Judah a different way and not to eat bread or water.

The man of God was stopped on his way home, by an older prophet, who lied to him and said that an angel had said to him that it was alright for him to eat bread and drink water. This lie cost the man of God his life. A lion killed him.

This is a very strong lesson, which Paul would have been aware of. When we stand before God, we will not be able to bring the people who would discourage us with us. In the final analysis we need our works to be established by our faith. What do we believe?

Chapter 5

Finding My Cross

As a young child one of my favorite hymns was *'There is a green hill far away'*.

It continues -- *outside a city wall, where our dear Lord was crucified, who died to save us all.*

(Written by Cecil Frances Alexander (1818-1895), 1848 Music by: Horsley (William Horsley, 1774-1858)

I would sing the song and cry at the thought of Jesus suffering for me.

Now as a young Christian, 20 years old, I was to find that the way of the cross was for all of us.

"Martin, I think the Lord is saying to you that He wants you to lay down your clarinet."

This is without doubt the hardest word God has ever given to me. It was a friend, Alexander Blair, that brought the word to me. As I heard the word my body tried to be sick on the floor. My mind, soul and body could not cope with the communication. The clarinet had been my whole life, I practiced until I bled, I had won competitions and prizes at all stages of my playing. I was to embark on a career as a soloist, I already had an agent.

I still feel the pain, writing this now.

Before Alexander had given the word to me, another friend had given a word to me. This word was saying something quite different, but when I was listening to her it was if I was hearing 'Martin, I want you to lay the clarinet down.' As the word was more cryptic, I did not have to accept it, but when Alexander gave me the word in plain English I could not dodge the bullet, it was a confirmation.

I had already been given a word that God was going to use my playing to touch many people, so being asked to lay the clarinet down was going to be just for a season. Understanding this I still had to find an answer for God.

After searching my heart for a week I found that I could not lay the clarinet down. I could not pretend to lay it down, waiting for an angel to stop me, as was done for Abraham. Abraham must have had the intention to give his only begotten son, being fully committed to offering him to God.

I prayed – 'Dear Father, You have asked me to lay down the clarinet, and I can't. But I am willing for you to change my heart so that I am able to.'

A couple of days later, after praying the prayer, I was studying my Bible when I realized that I had forgotten to practice. This was impossible, as a classical musician I had gone for years and years practicing every day for many hours.

The Lord had helped me to lay the clarinet down and now my discipline and love was turned to the word of God. I loved the Bible, and studied it incessantly.

The Lord said to me that my music career would be different from others, and that I would be playing my clarinet later in life, and that when I did He would heal people as I played.

(This word is now coming to fruition, I stopped playing the clarinet regularly 28 years ago, I am now playing again since April 2011 and people have reported healings of scoliosis, cancer, depression, injures from motorbike accidents, walking difficulties, bone problems, emotional inner healings, kidney stone disappearing.. etc.. Some experienced heat in their bodies as they were healed.)

The church I was attending 'Maranatha' was very strong in the Word. The importance of a firm foundation was emphasized, indeed the founder Bob Weiner and his wife Rose wrote a study book 'Bible Studies for a Firm Foundation', which I heartily recommend to all lovers of the Word.

Chapter 6

An Arranged Marriage
(Walking in the Spirit)

O ne of the controversial teachings of the church that I attended, Maranatha, was a 'no dating' policy. When it was time for you to marry God would tell you.

Understanding that every women was either a sister or mother, with one chosen women to be a bride for me was perfect. There would be no need to try different women to find the one that fit.

One of the reasons I had been drawn back to my Father, God, was that I had gone through the pain of failed relationships. I wanted what my parents had, a marriage arranged by God.

Another benefit of the teaching, was that for the first time I could appreciate how to love a women as a sister. I had grown up in a family of men, two brothers and no sisters. Girls had always been objects of romance, not friends. Being released to love them as sisters was a new thing for me. Suddenly, relationships to the opposite sex, was based on purity, wanting to care for them, wanting the best for them. So, I waited to see who my Father would give me as a wife.

"Martin, you are getting married soon". I had just laid my head on my pillow, God would often talk to me just as I laid down.

Approximately two weeks passed.

"Martin, you are getting engaged soon." "What is the name of the girl?" I enquired.
Very loudly, I heard "Janet". She was a very pretty girl attending the church. I had never had a conversation with her, just a simple 'hello'. In utter amazement I replied 'No', as in 'how can it be?' I received a very strong reply of "Janet". The tone of the voice was with such authority, an unquestionable timbre. I got up from my bed in bewilderment, went to the bathroom looked in the mirror and said to myself "I'm marrying, Janet".

The next morning I spoke to my elder brother Seamus. "Seamus, last night God told me that I was going to marry a girl called 'Janet'." Seamus looked at me, not being a Christian, he said in a manner that only an older brother could. "Martin, has all that studying, gone to your head?"
I didn't care, he would find out, I was going to marry 'Janet'.

I called Janet on the phone that day. "Could I come around for dinner?" I asked. "Yes", she replied "how about Tuesday?"

Janet also invited a girlfriend to the meal, as she wanted some morale support. Janet already knew why I was coming. Three months earlier she had been praying about who she would marry. The Lord gave her an open vision of me standing in front of her. She then prayed that God would bring it about, that she would do nothing to instigate it, not telling a soul. It was a surprise to her as she had always thought that I would marry a musician. We did not mix in the same circle of friends.

At the meal, nothing was said about relationships, afterwards we all prayed together.
After I had left, Janet's friend Louise said to that it was strange, because when she had been praying she had felt as if she was praying for us as a couple.

I went on to see Janet every day that week, and before the week was over we were engaged.

Three months later on August 23rd 1986 we were married at St. John's Church, Old Woking, Surrey, England.

We have now been married twenty five years, with two beautiful children, David and Sophia.

When God gives you a wife He knows what the future holds for you, and when you give that area of your life into His hands, He chooses the perfect soul mate for you.

I love working for God.

Talents Music Shop

Having a wife to support, I needed to find work. This was strange to me, having studied for so long to be a soloist, it had never occurred to me that I would have to work, in the conventional sense of the word.

I became a salesman for 'Charterhouse Woodwind and Brass'. This was a big come down for me. I had played as a soloist in the major concert halls of England, and now I was working in a music store. I was earning very, very little money, and was starting to moan a little to God about it.

"Martin, you are looking at this the wrong way." God said to me.
"Instead of seeing it as they are paying you little money to work for them. You need to see that they are training you up to own a music store, and you are not paying them for that."

Indeed I was learning how to run a music store and they were 'giving me' pocket money, a car and the gas to run it. It is interesting how we can look at things from a different perspective.

After a few more months Charterhouse went out of business, they went bankrupt.
Out of a job, I waited on what God would do next.

"Martin, I am going to give you a music shop." The Lord said.
"Lord, I don't have any money, how will that happen." I replied.
"Do what you can and I will do the rest" He said.

I think this is one of the keys to accomplishing works in the Kingdom of God. 'Do what you can, and He will do the rest'. When Jesus multiplied the loaves and the fish to provide for the 5,000 men and their women and children, the disciples had to do what they could. i.e. provide 5 loaves and 2 fishes.

How we obtained the Music shop is quite complicated, so I will simplify it a bit.

Having no money, there were some things I could do that would not cost anything.
I went to the estate agents, (realtors), and asked for information on their shops for sale.
I went to the banks and said I was opening a shop, and wanted to know who would give me the best deal.

We found a perfect shop, it was a Victorian, purpose built fish shop, with accommodation above.
It would need a lot of work, but it had everything we needed.

The man selling the shop owned a 12 year lease on the building, but did not own the freehold.
I felt that I needed to buy the freehold as well, so that we would completely own the building, but he wouldn't tell me who owned it. He said that he would tell me after I had put an offer for his lease.

"Lord, what shall I do?" I enquired.
The Lord told me to put an offer on the lease.

The leaseholder wanted 32,000 pounds for the lease, at the time 53,000 US dollars.
I did not have any money, but I didn't need any money to simply make an offer.

I offered him 28,000 pounds, (46,000 dollars), for the lease which he accepted.
He then gave me the telephone number of the man who owned the freehold.

"Lord, what shall I do now?" I enquired.
"Put an offer on the freehold." He replied.

Sometimes when I tell this testimony, people think that I was just a businessman making a deal.
But normal people don't go around putting offers on buildings without any money. In fact, I could not bring myself to telephone the freeholder. The only way I could summon up the courage was to have my wife pray in the spirit as I rang him.

"Mr. Leopard, I am buying the lease on 9 Brockley Rise, and would like to buy your freehold."
" Okay, he replied". He had already been in negotiations with the leaseholder, for him to buy it.
" I want 28,500 pounds for it." (47,000 dollars at the time). I was astonished, the price when added to the cost of the lease, came to approximately one third to half of the value of the building. Mr. Leopard then went on to give me the address of his lawyer, and I never spoke to him again.

When you have no income, it is very difficult to get a mortgage. This is what I was finding out.

When I had earlier telephoned the banks, one bank manager had suggested that I get a business development loan, as a way of starting the business. I thought that I would try that avenue, even though it would be at a higher interest rate. He asked me to bring my accounts and bank statements. I said that I didn't have any accounts made up, so he simply asked me to bring my bank statements. As you can imagine, without any income the statements looked pretty bad, always overdrawn.

The day of the meeting with the bank manager arrived, it was a sunny spring day. Having outlined the business plan to him, he asked for my bank statements. Handing the statements to him, I internally cried out to God.

"That's fine, Mr. Powell." The bank manager said, handing them back to me. I am not sure what happened, why he thought they were 'fine'. But I didn't question it.

The bank manager called his assistant in to prepare a loan form for me. He agreed to lend me 56,000 pounds, (92,000 dollars). The repayments were going to be around 650 pounds a month, and I had 84 pounds a month coming in.

Realizing there was going to be a short fall, I was praying what to do.

"I'm going to need a business overdraft." I said.
Looking into my eyes the bank manager said "How much do you want?"
"20,000 pounds" (33,000 dollars) I replied.
"That seems fine to me." He replied.
He called his assistant in again and asked her to open a bank account for me with the overdraft facility agreed.

The bank manager lent me the money to buy the building, and

then lent me the money to pay him back with.

In all of this, I had never met this man before, just two conversations on the phone, I did not bank with them.

A group of my friends came together and we asked the Lord the name of the business. My friend Richard Storry heard a word 'Talents', and Talents Music Shop was born.

Chapter 7

King David

King David showed great intimacy with God. This is demonstrated in the psalms that he wrote, up to 78 of the psalms are thought to have been written by David. One can imagine him, using his memories of being a shepherd writing the 23 psalm.

> The LORD *is* my shepherd; I shall not want. ² He maketh me to lie down in green pastures: he leadeth me beside the still waters. ³ He restoreth my soul: he leadeth me in the paths of righteousness for his name's sake. ⁴ Yea, though I walk through the valley of the shadow of death, I will fear no evil: for thou *art* with me; thy rod and thy staff they comfort me. ⁵ Thou preparest a table before me in the presence of mine enemies: thou anointest my head with oil; my cup runneth over. ⁶ Surely goodness and mercy shall follow me all the days of my life: and I will dwell in the house of the LORD for ever. (Psalm 23 KJV)

The heartfelt remorse felt at letting God down, after committing adultery with Bathsheba and causing her husband Uriah to be killed.

A Psalm of David, when Nathan the prophet came unto him, after he had gone in to Bathsheba.

> Have mercy upon me, O God, according to thy lovingkindness: according unto the multitude of thy tender mercies blot out my transgressions. ² Wash me throughly from mine iniquity, and cleanse me from my sin. ³ For I acknowledge my transgressions: and my sin *is* ever before me. ⁴ Against thee, thee only, have I sinned, and done *this* evil in thy sight: that thou mightest be justified when thou speakest, *and* be clear when thou judgest. ⁵ Behold, I was shapen in iniquity; and in sin did my mother conceive me. ⁶ Behold, thou desirest truth in the inward parts: and in the hidden *part* thou shalt make me to know wisdom. ⁷ Purge me with hyssop, and I shall be clean: wash me, and I shall be whiter than snow. ⁸ Make me to hear joy and gladness; *that* the bones *which* thou hast broken may rejoice. ⁹ Hide thy face from my sins, and blot out all mine iniquities. ¹⁰ Create in me a clean heart, O God; and renew a right spirit within me. ¹¹ Cast me not away from thy presence; and take not thy holy spirit from me. ¹² Restore unto me the joy of thy salvation; and uphold me *with thy* free spirit. ¹³ *Then* will I teach transgressors thy ways; and sinners shall be converted unto thee. ¹⁴ Deliver me from bloodguiltiness, O God, thou God of my salvation: *and* my tongue shall sing aloud of thy righteousness. ¹⁵ O Lord, open thou my lips; and my mouth shall shew forth thy praise. ¹⁶ For thou desirest not sacrifice; else would I give *it*: thou

delightest not in burnt offering. [17] The sacrifices of God *are* a broken spirit: a broken and a contrite heart, O God, thou wilt not despise. [18] Do good in thy good pleasure unto Zion: build thou the walls of Jerusalem. [19] Then shalt thou be pleased with the sacrifices of righteousness, with burnt offering and whole burnt offering: then shall they offer bullocks upon thine altar. (Psalm 51 KJV)

This intimacy and relationship with God is characterized by David's communication with God.

Many times in scripture David enquiries of the Lord, to see what he should do. Let us have a look at some of them.

In this first portion of scripture we read about how David responds to hearing that his fellow Israelites were being attacked at Keilah.

Then they told David, saying, Behold, the Philistines fight against Keilah, and they rob the threshingfloors. [2] Therefore **David enquired of the LORD, saying, Shall I go and smite these Philistines? And the LORD said unto David, Go, and smite the Philistines, and save Keilah.** [3] And David's men said unto him, Behold, we be afraid here in Judah: how much more then if we come to Keilah against the armies of the Philistines? [4] Then **David enquired of the LORD yet again. And the LORD answered him and said, Arise, go down to Keilah; for I will deliver the Philistines into thine hand.** [5] So David and his men went to Keilah, and fought with the Philistines, and brought away their cattle, and smote them with a great slaughter. So David saved the inhabitants of Keilah. (1 Samuel 23:1-5)

David enquired twice about whether to go and fight against the Philistines at Keilah, and twice the Lord said to fight them and save Keilah.

After a great slaughter, David saved the inhabitants of Keilah. So you would think that these people would love David and treat him like a hero.

Keilah was a walled city with gates and bars. King Saul, wanting to kill David, realized that David would be trapped in the city if he attacked it with his army. David would be safe in a walled city though, wouldn't he? David enquired of the Lord.

> Then said David, O LORD God of Israel, thy servant hath certainly heard that Saul seeketh to come to Keilah, to destroy the city for my sake. [11] Will the men of Keilah deliver me up into his hand? will Saul come down, as thy servant hath heard? O LORD God of Israel, I beseech thee, tell thy servant. And the LORD said, **He will come down.** [12] Then said David, Will the men of Keilah deliver me and my men into the hand of Saul? And the LORD said, **They will deliver *thee* up.** [13] Then David and his men, *which were* about six hundred, arose and departed out of Keilah, and went whithersoever they could go. And it was told Saul that David was escaped from Keilah; and he forbare to go forth. (1 Samuel 23:10-13)

Even though David and his men had saved Keilah from the Philistines, they would have delivered them up to Saul. Thank goodness David did not assume that the people of Keilah would protect him.

Later when David and his men returned to their home town

of Ziklag, they found that the city had been burnt and their wives, and children had been taken captive. David enquired of the Lord, what to do.

> And David was greatly distressed; for the people spake of stoning him, because the soul of all the people was grieved, every man for his sons and for his daughters: but David encouraged himself in the LORD his God. ⁷ And David said to Abiathar the priest, Ahimelech's son, I pray thee, bring me hither the ephod. And Abiathar brought thither the ephod to David. ⁸ And David enquired at the LORD, saying, Shall I pursue after this troop? shall I overtake them? And he answered him, **Pursue: for thou shalt surely overtake *them*, and without fail recover *all*.** (1 Samuel 30:6-8)

> And David smote them from the twilight even unto the evening of the next day: and there escaped not a man of them, save four hundred young men, which rode upon camels, and fled. ¹⁸ And David recovered all that the Amalekites had carried away: and David rescued his two wives. ¹⁹ And **there was nothing lacking to them**, neither small nor great, neither sons nor daughters, neither spoil, nor any *thing* that they had taken to them: **David recovered all.** (1 Samuel 30:17-19)

David's love for God was so great that he wanted to build a temple for him. God wouldn't let David build the temple, because he had spilt so much blood as a man of war. But God said that Solomon his son would build it. But David didn't just let it go at that, he collected tremendous amounts of gold, silver, iron, bronze, marble, wood and precious stones for the building of the temple. Also he wrote down the plans of how the temple should be built, let us see how he did that. Read 1 Chronicles chapter 28 and 29.

> Then David gave to Solomon his son the pattern of the porch, and of the houses thereof, and of the treasuries thereof, and of the upper chambers thereof, and of the inner parlours thereof, and of the place of the mercy seat, ¹² And **the pattern of all that he had by the spirit**, of the courts of the house of the LORD, and of all the chambers round about, of the treasuries of the house of God, and of the treasuries of the dedicated things: (1 Chronicles 28:11-12)

David received the pattern of these things by the spirit.

> All *this, said David*, **the LORD made me understand in writing** by *his* **hand upon me**, *even* all the works of this pattern. (1 Chronicles 28:19)

Can we see here that in the same way as we are writing down our journals of what God is saying to us by his Spirit, so in like manner David received the pattern to build the temple by the Spirit writing it down with God's hand upon him. The same method!!

I hope everyone is writing down their words from God, testing the spirits.

When you first write down the words you hear, it may be that you only hear one word.

I remember I was invited to minister at Holy Trinity Brompton, London. I was giving words to a number of people and out of the blue, I was given a single word 'party'.

It would have been very easy to discount the word, and not mention it. But, I knew that I had heard it. I decided that I would give the single word 'party'. As I did, a couple burst out laughing. The husband was in a wheelchair, and they had been contemplating having a party 'in faith' to celebrate his healing before the healing was manifest. If I hadn't given the word, then they would not have received the encouragement that their plans were known in heaven.

Do not despise prophecy, even one single word.

Another way to encourage your ability to listen, is to ask God for words to give to other people.

Remember --

> Give, and it shall be given unto you; good measure, pressed down, and shaken together, and running over, shall men give into your bosom. For with the same measure that ye mete withal it shall be measured to you again. **(Luke 6:38)**

As we give words to other people, God multiplies words back to us.

Let us pray: (Get your pens and computers ready)

'Dear Lord, I want to be a servant that listens to your Voice. Is there anybody that you would like me to give a word to for You? (Often that person will come into your mind at this point.) What would you like me to say to them? Please help me to write them a note. In the name of Jesus. Amen.'

I was doing this exercise myself one day, writing a letter to someone.

It started—Dear Alison, ... etc..

The letter went on for about an A4 page. When I had finished I said "Lord, which Alison is this for, I know four Alisons?" He replied "Alison Little". I said to Him that I did not know an Alison Little. Later on I was introduced to a lady, her name was Alison Little. I was able to say, 'Oh, by the way I have a letter for you from God', and then gave it to her.

I guess the letter would have made an impact on her, as I had never heard of her.

A similar testimony, where the Lord has given me someone's name, was when I needed a new guitar teacher for my music store. Our present guitar teacher was moving on, and we needed a new teacher. Getting a good teacher, can be a problem, but when they get a recommendation from God they must be good.

"Lord, who shall I get to teach the guitar?" I asked. "Malcolm MacFarlane" He replied.

Well, I didn't know anybody with that name. I decided to have a look in the Musician Union handbook of music teachers for Great Britain. Looking down the list of guitar teachers I found one called Malcolm MacFarlane. He lived approximately one mile from the store in London.
I rang him up, and he came and taught the guitar at our store for a number of years.

Chapter 8

The Major Prophets
and the Voice

L et us examine the Major Prophets, the experts. How they heard God speak to them, and what we can learn from their lives.

Isaiah

Isaiah's name: יְשַׁעְיָה Yesha`yah

Meaning: Isaiah or Jesaiah or Jeshaiah = "Jehovah has saved"

Isaiah prophesied during the reign of four Kings of Judah-- Uzziah, Jotham, Ahaz, and Hezekiah.
This was a turbulent period of time, God was not happy with His people. This theme, is shown to us very early from verse 2 of chapter 1.

> Hear, O heavens, and give ear, O earth: for the
> LORD hath spoken, I have nourished and brought
> up children, and they have rebelled against me. ³
> The ox knoweth his owner, and the ass his master's
> crib: *but* **Israel doth not know, my people doth**
> **not consider.** ⁴ Ah sinful nation, a people laden
> with iniquity, a seed of evildoers, children that are
> corrupters: they have forsaken the LORD, they have
> provoked the Holy One of Israel unto anger, they
> are gone away backward. (Isaiah 1:2-4)

Not only were his children, Israel, backsliding and rebelling, it
seems they were not even aware that they were doing it. God
explains to them that the reason the country is suffering is
because of their rebellion. He likens their leaders to the leaders
of Sodom and Gomorrah and exhorts them to 'Hear the Word'
and give attention to the written law. This follows our guidelines
in hearing Gods voice, it will always agree with His written word.

> Hear the word of the LORD, ye rulers of Sodom;
> give ear unto the law of our God, ye people of
> Gomorrah. (Isaiah 1:10)

God does not hold back in how he accurately describes Jerusalem.

> How is the faithful city become an harlot! it was full
> of judgment; righteousness lodged in it; but now
> murderers. (Isaiah 1:21)

Appealing to Israel to come close to Him and reason together,
God clearly explains the choices and the ramifications of each
choice.

> Come now, and let us reason together, saith the
> LORD: though your sins be as scarlet, they shall be as

white as snow; though they be red like crimson, they shall be as wool. ¹⁹ If ye be willing and obedient, ye shall eat the good of the land: ²⁰ But if ye refuse and rebel, ye shall be devoured with the sword: for the mouth of the LORD hath spoken *it*. (Isaiah 1:18-20 KJV)

Willingness and obedience would result in 'eating the good of the land' – blessings. Refusal and rebellion would result in destruction.

This opening chapter of Isaiah, full of exasperation, anger and words of destruction, is followed in chapter two by hope, what God has planned for Judah and Jerusalem in the last days.

And it shall come to pass in the last days, *that* the mountain of the LORD'S house shall be established in the top of the mountains, and shall be exalted above the hills; and all nations shall flow unto it. ³ And many people shall go and say, Come ye, and let us go up to the mountain of the LORD, to the house of the God of Jacob; and he will teach us of his ways, and we will walk in his paths: for out of Zion shall go forth the law, and the word of the LORD from Jerusalem. ⁴ And he shall judge among the nations, and shall rebuke many people: and they shall beat their swords into plowshares, and their spears into pruninghooks: nation shall not lift up sword against nation, neither shall they learn war any more. (Isaiah 2:2-4)

This prophecy has obviously not happened yet, as the nations are still fighting. But doesn't it give the amazing breadth of God's foresight, seeing the end from the beginning. It truly brings Solomon's words to life.

The end of a matter is better than its beginning; (Ecclesiastes 7:8 NASB)

The whole book of Isaiah could be summed up, as Isaiah's name indicates, in two sections—Judgment and Salvation. In chapter 53 we have the most stunning revelation of the author of our salvation Jesus.

It is worth looking at Isaiah's revelation of Heaven.

> In the year that king Uzziah died I saw also the Lord sitting upon a throne, high and lifted up, and his train filled the temple. ² Above it stood the seraphims: each one had six wings; with twain he covered his face, and with twain he covered his feet, and with twain he did fly. ³ And one cried unto another, and said, Holy, holy, holy, *is* the LORD of hosts: the whole earth *is* full of his glory. ⁴ And the posts of the door moved at the voice of him that cried, and the house was filled with smoke. ⁵ Then said I, Woe *is* me! for I am undone; because I *am* a man of unclean lips, and I dwell in the midst of a people of unclean lips: for mine eyes have seen the King, the LORD of hosts. ⁶ Then flew one of the seraphims unto me, having a live coal in his hand, *which* he had taken with the tongs from off the altar: ⁷ And he laid *it* upon my mouth, and said, Lo, this hath touched thy lips; and thine iniquity is taken away, and thy sin purged. ⁸ **Also I heard the voice of the Lord, saying, Whom shall I send, and who will go for us? Then said I, Here *am* I; send me.** ⁹ And he said, Go, and tell this people, Hear ye indeed, but understand not; and see ye indeed, but perceive not. ¹⁰ Make the heart of this people fat, and make their ears heavy, and shut their eyes; lest they see with their eyes, and hear with their

ears, and understand with their heart, and convert, and be healed. (Isaiah 6:1-10)

Hearing the Voice of the Lord, Isaiah responded, saying 'Hear am I; send me.'

We must pray:

Dear Father, It is our heartfelt cry to respond to you. You have asked 'whom shall I send' Lord, send us. Give us our missions and the strength to accomplish all you have for us. I ask this in the name of Jesus. Amen.

Although in this book we are primarily looking at 'listening' to the Voice of God, let us note how Isaiah was able to 'see' into the heavenly realm. God hasn't just given us a spirit that can hear, but also one that can 'see' in the spirit as well. We will look at 'seeing' in chapter 11.

Jeremiah

Jeremiah's name: יִרְמְיָה Yirmeyah or יִרְמְיָהוּ Yirmeyahuw {yir-meh-yaw'-hoo}

Meaning: Jeremiah = "whom Jehovah has appointed"

Isaiah prophesied during the reign of four Kings of Judah-- Uzziah, Jotham, Ahaz, and Hezekiah.
This was a turbulent period of time, God was not happy with His people. This theme, is shown to us very early from verse 2 of chapter 1.

Jeremiah prophesied during the reigns three Kings of Judah--

Josiah, Jehoiakim, and Zedekiah. This wast a time when the Judgments on Judah were coming to a fulfillment. Israel had come out of Egypt under Moses, and now they had come a full circle and those left in Jerusalem were going to go back to Egypt.

Early in the book of Jeremiah we see that he was destined to be a prophet.

> "Before I formed you in the womb I knew you; Before you were born I sanctified you; I ordained you a prophet to the nations." ⁶ Then said I: "Ah, Lord GOD! Behold, I cannot speak, for I *am* a youth." ⁷ But the LORD said to me: "Do not say, 'I *am* a youth,' For you shall go to all to whom I send you, And whatever I command you, you shall speak. ⁸ Do not be afraid of their faces, For I *am* with you to deliver you," says the LORD. ⁹ Then the LORD put forth His hand and touched my mouth, and the LORD said to me: "Behold, I have put My words in your mouth. ¹⁰ See, I have this day set you over the nations and over the kingdoms, To root out and to pull down, To destroy and to throw down, To build and to plant." (Jeremiah 1:5-10 NKJV)

Notice how Jeremiah was told not to be afraid. Fear is a major weapon in our adversaries armory. Do not allow fear to paralyze you from obeying the voice of God.

Over and over again we read in Jeremiah how God's people would not obey his voice.

> 'Return, backsliding Israel,' says the LORD; 'I will not cause My anger to fall on you. For I *am* merciful,' says the LORD; 'I will not remain angry forever.

[13] Only acknowledge your iniquity, That you have transgressed against the LORD your God, And have scattered your charms To alien deities under every green tree, And *you have not obeyed My voice,*' says the LORD. (Jeremiah 3:12-13 NKJV)

We have sinned against the LORD our God, We and our fathers, From our youth even to this day, *And have not obeyed the voice of the LORD our God.*" (Jeremiah 3:25 NKJV)

We can see that God get's quite frustrated with them and says quite plainly that they cannot see or hear.

'Hear this now, O foolish people, Without understanding, Who have eyes and see not, And who have ears and hear not: (Jeremiah 5:21 NKJV)

Obey My voice, and I will be your God, and you shall be My people. And walk in all the ways that I have commanded you, *that it may be well with you.*' [24] "Yet they did not obey or incline their ear, but followed the counsels *and* the dictates of their evil hearts, and went backward and not forward. [25] "Since the day that your fathers came out of the land of Egypt until this day, I have even sent to you all My servants the prophets, daily rising up early and sending *them.* [26] "Yet they did not obey Me or incline their ear, but stiffened their neck. They did worse than their fathers. [27] " Therefore you shall speak all these words to them, but they will not obey you. You shall also call to them, but they will not answer you. [28] "So you shall say to them, 'This *is* a nation that does not obey the voice of the LORD their God nor receive correction. (Jeremiah 7:23-28 NKJV)

When fear and unbelief comes into our hearts we forget that when God is speaking to us it is that 'it may be will well with us'. He is trying to bless us, but we refuse, believing and trusting in our own hearts.

The major theme of the book of Jeremiah is 'listening to the Voice', we see from chapters 42-43 of the book that they wanted to hear the voice, but did not believe and obey the voice, returning to Egypt.

Now all the captains of the forces, ... and all the people, from the least to the greatest, came near ² and said to Jeremiah the prophet, "Please, ... pray for us to the LORD your God..... ³ "that the LORD your God may show us the way in which we should walk and the thing we should do." ···· ⁶ "Whether *it is* pleasing or displeasing, we will obey the voice of the LORD our God ·······"Thus says the LORD, the God of Israel, ... ¹⁰ 'If you will still remain in this land, then I will build you and not pull *you* down.... **43:1** Now it happened, when Jeremiah had stopped ... ² that ... all the proud men spoke, saying to Jeremiah, "You speak falsely! The LORD our God has not sent you to say, 'Do not go to Egypt to dwell there.' ····⁴ So Johanan the son of Kareah, all the captains of the forces, and all the people would not obey the voice of the LORD, to remain in the land of Judah...... ⁷ So they went to the land of Egypt, for they did not obey the voice of the LORD. (Jeremiah 42:1 - 43:7 NKJV)

Have you noticed in people's lives, that they often repeat the same mistakes and their lives go around in circles. Let us not be like those who returned to Egypt.

Let's pray.

Dear Father we want to be children that bring you pleasure, if we have heard your voice and disobeyed please forgive us.

Remind me of the words you have spoken to be me that I have not believed and obeyed. Be gracious to me, cleanse me from fear and unbelief, give me faith and remind me of those words that I may complete the missions given into my hands. I ask this in the name of Jesus. Amen.

Ezekiel

Ezekiel's name: יחזקאל Yechezqe'l

Meaning: Ezekiel or Jehezekel = "God strengthens"

Ezekiel prophesied from among the captives by the river Chebar, he was among those exiled to Babylon.

Operating as a 'watchman', Ezekiel sees into the heavenly realms, teaches us the responsibilities, contends with 'false' prophets, and gives hope of a new temple and Kingdom.

In chapter one of Ezekiel, he is given a vision of 'the likeness of the glory of the LORD'.
This glimpse into the heavenly is repeated later in chapter 43, and Ezekiel is also given a vision of a new temple where he will 'dwell... for ever.

> And he said unto me, Son of man, the place of my throne, and the place of the soles of my feet, where I will dwell in the midst of the children of Israel *for ever*, (Ezekiel 43:7)

Where we read in Isaiah, and Jeremiah, about the judgments upon Israel, we now see in Ezekiel the hope stored up.

Let us read from chapter 3, below, the responsibilities of a watchmen.

> Son of man, I have made thee a watchman unto the house of Israel: therefore hear the word at my mouth, and give them warning from me. [18] When I say unto the wicked, Thou shalt surely die; and thou givest him not warning, nor speakest to warn the wicked from his wicked way, to save his life; the same wicked *man* shall die in his iniquity; but his blood will I require at thine hand. [19] Yet if thou warn the wicked, and he turn not from his wickedness, nor from his wicked way, he shall die in his iniquity; but thou hast delivered thy soul. [20] Again, When a righteous *man* doth turn from his righteousness, and commit iniquity, and I lay a stumblingblock before him, he shall die: because thou hast not given him warning, he shall die in his sin, and his righteousness which he hath done shall not be remembered; but his blood will I require at thine hand. [21] Nevertheless if thou warn the righteous *man*, that the righteous sin not, and he doth not sin, he shall surely live, because he is warned; also thou hast delivered thy soul. (Ezekiel 3:17-21)

Not all of us who prophesy are called to be 'watchmen'. But I believe the principle is the same.

It is important that when we hear a word for someone, that we deliver that word. Otherwise we may end up being responsible. It is also important for the person receiving the word to test the word, as we do not want to be false prophets.

Recently I received a word for a friend of mine that he had some big decisions coming up, and that if he made the wrong choice he would die. This was a very uncomfortable word to receive, and I didn't want to give him the word. But I also did not want him to die, and if he did be responsible for it. I gave him the word with the warning to test the word, and then I made sure that I prayed for him that he would make the right decisions.

As we pass on the words given to us for others, then God will give us more.

Let us not forget the principle that when we are faithful with little, God gives us more.

> His lord said unto him, Well done, *thou* good and faithful servant: thou hast been faithful over a few things, I will make thee ruler over many things: enter thou into the joy of thy lord. (Matthew 25:21)

Ezekiel's ministry, as a watchman, also entailed contending with false prophets.

> And the word of the LORD came to me, saying, ² "Son of man, prophesy against the prophets of Israel who prophesy, and say to those who *prophesy out of their own heart*, 'Hear the word of the LORD!' " ³ …. "Woe to the foolish prophets, who *follow their own spirit* and have seen nothing…. ⁶ "They have envisioned futility and false divination, saying, 'Thus says the LORD!' But the LORD has not sent them; yet *they hope that the word may be confirmed.* ⁷ "Have you not seen a futile vision, and have you not spoken false divination? You say, 'The LORD says,' but I have not spoken." ⁸ Therefore thus says the Lord GOD: "Because you have spoken nonsense and envisioned lies, therefore I *am* indeed against you," says the Lord GOD. ⁹ "My hand will be against the prophets who

envision futility and who divine lies; they shall not be in the assembly of My people, nor be written in the record of the house of Israel, nor shall they enter into the land of Israel. Then you shall know that I *am* the Lord GOD. ¹⁰ "Because, indeed, because they have seduced My people, saying, 'Peace!' when *there is* no peace. (Ezekiel 13:1-16 NKJV)

We can see, from the scriptures above, that false prophets are hearing from their own hearts, from their own spirits. It is not necessarily that they are not hearing a voice, it is that they are not hearing the Voice of the Holy Spirit. That is why it is of upmost importance to test every spirit, and test the words you are hearing.

Beloved, do not believe every spirit, but test the spirits, whether they are of God; because many false prophets have gone out into the world. (1 John 4:1 NKJV)

Let two or three prophets speak, and let the others judge. (1 Corinthians 14:29 NKJV)

Do not despise prophecies. ²¹ Test all things; hold fast what is good. (1 Thessalonians 5:20-21 NKJV)

It is better to be humble and say that one has heard a voice, then to claim 'Thus says the LORD', when it has not been proved.

Chapter 9

The New Haven Fellowship

Without doubt, the hardest and most rewarding work I have done is being a Pastor. Thank goodness for Jesus, without Him it would be impossible.

I remember clearly, I was sitting on a brown sofa in our living room. 'Lord, what church would you like us to attend?' Quite a simple question, it had been laid on my heart that we were going to be moving from our present church. I had not changed church since giving my life back to Jesus in 1981, ten years previously, but was aware that God was moving us on.

'Martin, I want you to start a Church.' The words came clearly into my heart.
'Lord, I'm too busy', was my immediate response, then realizing the incongruity of saying 'Lord', and 'too busy' in the same sentence.

When I gave my life to Jesus in 1981, it was without conditions, a complete surrender to His will. It was not my place to decide what to do with my life, as He had bought it, fully paid for on the cross. At this point in time, I was ready to Pastor a church, I had led home groups for 8 years, had taken 'foundations for ministry' courses, and would have no problem with leading worship. I had studied the piano at the Royal Academy of Music, for four years.

So the pertinent question was, 'is this the Lord speaking'? I knew it was not my flesh, I had no desire to be a Pastor. Though the Lord had told me as a child that I would be a preacher I had not tried to make anything happen. I had seen how hard it could be for Pastors. You cannot please all of the people all of the time, and you certainly cannot please the world and Satan, any of the time when you are building God's Kingdom.

'Lord would you please bring in the confirmations.' I asked.
Many of our friends were now praying into the project and all of the responses were that we were to do it. We were given many confirming words. I asked the Lord from whom we should get 'covering'? He responded 'John Linden-Cook'. John is the Pastor of Norwood Christian Fellowship, and regularly conducted healing campaigns and taught at Full Gospel Business Men's Fellowship International Teaching days.

Another of my friends 'Peter Clark' responded to me that he had been praying, and that the Lord told him that I should start the church and get 'covering' from John Linden-Cook.

He asked me whether I had heard of John, to which I responded that I indeed knew him and was already talking to him about 'covering'.

The final confirmation we had before starting the church, was from a friend who had seen a vision of a row of musical instruments all queued up outside the music store. They were all broken and needed mending. As we had already been told that the church was to be like a hospital, providing a haven for people to be mended, this last confirmation really touched our hearts. We had 'heard from the Lord', it was His will for us to start the church, and we did.

In 1998 the New Haven Fellowship became a member of Churches in Communities International, headed by Dr. Hugh Osgood.

Chapter 10

Elijah Versus Elisha

אֵלִיָּהוּ 'Eliyah {ay-lee-yaw'}
Meaning: Elijah or Eliah = "my God is Jehovah

אֱלִישָׁע 'Eliysha` {el-ee-shaw'}
Meaning: Elisha = "God is salvation"

In learning about 'listening to the Voice', I would like to highlight one of the differences between Elijah and Elisha.

Both of these Prophets demonstrated the power of God in the miraculous, but one of them was greater.

Whilst Isaiah, Jeremiah, and Ezekiel, wrote God's words, Elijah and Elisha demonstrated the power of God. The miracles that were displayed in their lives were a foreshadow of the miracles of our Lord Jesus—The dead raised, miracles of provision, lepers cleansed.

When we look at the recorded miracles performed by Elijah and Elisha we note that Elisha performed approximately twice as many miracles as Elijah.

Many teachers point to the fact that Elisha asked for a double portion of Elijah's spirit.

> And so it was, when they had crossed over, that Elijah said to Elisha, "Ask! What may I do for you, before I am taken away from you?" Elisha said, "Please let a double portion of your spirit be upon me." (2 Kings 2:9 NKJV)

Let us examine how they died.

When it was time for Elijah to pass over, he was taken up to heaven in a chariot of fire.

> And it came to pass, as they still went on, and talked, that, behold, *there appeared* a chariot of fire, and horses of fire, and parted them both asunder; and Elijah went up by a whirlwind into heaven. [12] And Elisha saw *it*, and he cried, My father, my father, the chariot of Israel, and the horsemen thereof. (2 Kings 2:11-12)

Incidentally whilst I was in a prayer meeting, held by Ann Rountree in Moravian Falls N.C, I saw a chariot of fire. I saw the angel in the chariot wielding a whip made from fire. It is quite amazing to see something made out of fire.

Elijah was greatly honored to be taken up in a chariot of fire. So as Elisha performed twice as many miracles as Elijah one could assume that he would be given a similar honor.

When it was time for Elisha to die, he was with King Joash, who expressed the assumption that the chariot of fire would come for Elisha, even using the same words that Elisha had uttered when Elijah was taken. But Elisha was not taken he was buried.

> Now Elisha was fallen sick of his sickness whereof he died. And Joash the king of Israel came down unto him, and wept over his face, and said, O my father, my father, the chariot of Israel, and the horsemen thereof.…. [20] And Elisha died, and they buried him. (2 Kings 13:14-20)

Elisha died of a sickness. How could such an anointed man of God die of a sickness, had the anointing left him?

> And Elisha died, and they buried him. And the bands of the Moabites invaded the land at the coming in of the year. [21] And it came to pass, as they were burying a man, that, behold, they spied a band *of men*; and they cast the man into the sepulchre of Elisha: and when the man was let down, and touched the bones of Elisha, **he revived, and stood up on his feet**. (2 Kings 13:19-21)

Astonishingly the power of God was so strong in Elisha's bones, that a man was raised from the dead simply by touching them.

So why was Elisha not healed what had happened in his life that would give him such an ignominious end?

I think the clue can be found in two of the stories about Elisha's life.

> Then he went up from there to Bethel; and as he was going up by the way, young lads came out from the

city and mocked him and said to him, "Go up, you baldhead; go up, you baldhead!" ²⁴ When he looked behind him and saw them, he cursed them in the name of the LORD. Then two female bears came out of the woods and tore up forty-two lads of their number. (2 Kings 2:23-24 NAS)

To whom much is given much is expected. When we ask for the anointing and power of God we need to be careful how we use it. I must admit that I don't have the hair on my head that I had when I was young. But Elisha responded to teasing, by children, with a curse in the name of the Lord. This curse had consequences to those children and Elisha.

Also Elisha responded harshly in judgment to his servant Gehazi *and* his descendents. This can be found in 2 Kings chapter 5.

Gehazi had been a faithful servant to Elisha, but made a mistake in wanting a payment from Naaman for his healing, after Elisha had refused a payment.

Then he said to him, "Did not my heart go *with you* when the man turned back from his chariot to meet you? *Is it* time to receive money and to receive clothing, olive groves and vineyards, sheep and oxen, male and female servants? ²⁷ "Therefore the leprosy of Naaman shall cling to you and your descendants forever." And he went out from his presence leprous, *as white* as snow. (2 Kings 5:26-27 NKJV)

Gehazi was wrong, but love covers a multitude of sins. I have had people work for me in my business, when they make mistakes one tries to cover them.
Here Gehazi's mistake is not covered but is displayed all over his body, and the leprosy is given to his descendants 'forever'!

In this instance Elisha does not demonstrate love or discipline over his tongue.

We see that multitudes of miracles does not make us 'great'. Jesus commended John the Baptist saying that among those born of women there has not risen one greater, and then said that if we were willing to receive it, he is Elijah.

> "Assuredly, I say to you, among those born of women there has not risen one greater than John the Baptist; but he who is least in the kingdom of heaven is greater than he. [12] "And from the days of John the Baptist until now the kingdom of heaven suffers violence, and the violent take it by force. [13] "For all the prophets and the law prophesied until John. [14] "And if you are willing to receive *it,* he is Elijah who is to come. (Matthew 11:11-14 NKJ)

One of the byproducts of 'listening to the Voice', is that we will obtain more faith. Intimacy with God will always bring more faith simply as a fruit of the spirit.

> So then faith *comes* by hearing, and hearing by the word of God. (Romans 10:17 NKJV)

Listening to God produces faith, faith is released through our spoken words. As we grow in God's power we need to be careful that we do not curse people.

Looking at Elijah and Elisha gives us revelation on the motives of the heart.

When Elisha was asked what he wanted, he asked for a double portion of Elijah's spirit.

When Solomon was asked what he wanted, he asked for wisdom and knowledge to judge God's people. (found in 2 Chronicles 1:5)

The apostles asked Jesus to 'increase our faith'. Jesus explained that faith wasn't the problem but the motives of the heart-- That they needed the servant heart. (Found in Luke 17:5-10)

Let us pray:

Dear Father, we want to grow in listening to you, and obedience and faith follows on from hearing. Please Lord grant us the servants heart, that we may build your Kingdom and not our own. We ask this in the name of Jesus. Amen.

Chapter 11

Having Eyes to See

'**M**artin, what can you see?'

The question was posed yet again. This had been going on now for around about an hour.

I had started my quiet time as usual, sitting in front of my computer, writing to God, and waiting for replies. He asked me to close my eyes and tell Him what I could see. I could see the inside of my eyelids,

dark with spots of light. But the Lord, was not letting me stop. He persisted in asking me to look to see what I could see. I started praying in tongues, I wanted to focus in the spirit.

Suddenly I saw an arm raised with a knife, it was preparing to strike a man in his back. I saw the knife knocked out of the man's hand.

'Martin, do you know what caused that knife to be knocked out of the man's hand?' Jesus asked me.

'No, Lord.' I replied.

'It was your tongues, that knocked it out of the hand.' I was informed.

I loved praying in tongues, not as much as the Apostle Paul claimed he prayed, but how wonderful it was to realize that our prayers could be helping someone, perhaps on the other side of the world. How clever God is. I would not have thought to pray for that particular man, yet God could inspire me to pray for him through His Holy Spirit in an unknown tongue.

After waiting one hour to see this vision, after peering at spots and veins in my eyelids, I went on to see 21 visions in a row.

It made me wonder how many Christian brothers and sisters had tried to see in the spirit and would give up, before seeing anything. God's persistence in asking me to keep looking had paid off. I could now see more clearly in the spirit.

Later it occurred to me that I had been able to see certain things in the spirit, shortly after I had been baptized and filled with the Holy Spirit.

One Sunday morning in prayer, before going to church, the Lord said to me 'Martin I have given you a sword.' As He spoke I could clearly see the sword, as I moved my hand I could see the sword moving in the spirit with my hand. I could also see armor on each of my wrists.

I had read about the armor of God in Ephesians chapter six, but I hadn't realized that they were 'real' in the spirit.

Later that morning, I was at church. A friend called Sarah, approached me. 'Martin, the Lord asked me to tell you that He gave you a sword this morning.' 'I know' I replied. 'I have already seen it.'

I have since realized that God will often confirm what I have seen in the spirit. I suppose that He wants to encourage us that we are seeing 'correctly'.

Can we find this type of seeing in the scriptures?

> Moreover the word of the LORD came to me, saying, "Jeremiah, what do you see?" And I said, "I see a branch of an almond tree." [12] Then the LORD said to me, "You have seen well, for I am ready to perform My word." [13] And the word of the LORD came to me the second time, saying, "What do you see?" And I said, "I see a boiling pot, and it is facing away from the north." [14] Then the LORD said to me: "Out of the north calamity shall break forth On all the inhabitants of the land. (Jeremiah 1:11-14 NKJV)

> And the LORD said to me, "Amos, what do you see?" And I said, "A plumb line." Then the Lord said: "Behold, I am setting a plumb line In the midst of My people Israel; I will not pass by them anymore. (Amos 7:8 NKJV)

> Now the angel who talked with me came back and wakened me, as a man who is wakened out of his sleep. [2] And he said to me, "What do you see?" So I

said, "I am looking, and there *is* a lampstand of solid gold with a bowl on top of it, and on the *stand* seven lamps with seven pipes to the seven lamps. ³ "Two olive trees *are* by it, one at the right of the bowl and the other at its left." ⁴ So I answered and spoke to the angel who talked with me, saying, "What *are* these, my lord?" ⁵ Then the angel who talked with me answered and said to me, "Do you not know what these are?" And I said, "No, my lord." ⁶ So he answered and said to me: "This *is* the word of the LORD to Zerubbabel: 'Not by might nor by power, but by My Spirit,' Says the LORD of hosts. ⁷ 'Who *are* you, O great mountain? Before Zerubbabel *you shall become* a plain! And he shall bring forth the capstone With shouts of "Grace, grace to it!" ' " (Zechariah 4:1-7 NKJV)

I soon found out that not only could I see in the spirit, but also that it was possible to *fight* in the spirit.

I would go through the list of armor in Ephesians chapter six, then go and fight things that I could see in the spirit.

One day I was pondering, why my business was suffering from a lack of cash flow. As I was praying in the spirit I saw an octopus over the building. I decided to go and fight it in the spirit. I put my armor on and then attacked the spirit with my sword. I prayed continually in the spirit, asking the Holy spirit to guide my arm and sword as I was fighting. As one of the octopuses arms was cut off, I saw coins falling out of the wound. After approximately 15 minutes the Octopus was destroyed. The time was approximately one o'clock.

Later that day, a member of the church I Pastored asked me what I was doing at one o'clock.

I said that I had been fighting an unclean spirit. He said to me that he was crossing a road at one o'clock when the Holy Spirit said to him that he and another brother with him, were to urgently intercede for me as I was in spiritual warfare. They stopped at the side of the road and immediately interceded for the 15 minutes that I was in battle.

Again the Lord had confirmed to me what I was doing in the spirit from a source that was unaware I was going in to battle.

As the years progressed I would often go out in the spirit to fight. If I could not sleep, I would take that as a cue to fight from my bed. Some spirits are easy to fight, others harder, and some not to fight on your own.

Chapter 12

Fighting For the Life of My Son David

One of my favorite sayings is 'I love working for God'. I am always saying it, because I love working for God. I have never received a salary check all my working life.

When I was young in the Lord, He asked me one day 'Martin, is there anything you want?'

I pondered for half an hour without being able to think of anything I wanted. I then realized that He wasn't asking me if I wanted something, He was saying look I have given you everything.

Moved by this revelation I responded to God 'Lord, why have you given me so much?' He replied 'because I love you'. Sometimes we just don't understand that He loves us. One of Job's friends was named Bilhad, the translation of his name means 'confusing love'. Sometimes it may not appear to us that He loves us, that it is confusing love, but the fact is He still loves us whether we understand it or not.

Many years later I was praying and said to God that he had given me everything that I had wanted in life, but had not given me any children. Janet and myself had been married then for around fifteen years, and no children had come, we simply got on with our work in business and the church. Not long afterwards we found that Janet was pregnant.

Praise the living God, since 1986 when we were married I knew we would have a son called David, in fact both Janet and myself had had dreams where David was in them. He was expected and Janet was expecting.

David was born on the 11th March 2002 at Queen Mary's Hospital, Sidcup, South East London, England. It had been a difficult birth, Janet was in labor for 13 hours. Our joy soon turned to major concern. David was put into an incubator with wires and tubes all over him. He would not stop crying and we later learned he was not expected to last the night.

He had problems with his heart and brain.
The church was mobilized and everyone was praying. I asked if I could put my hands into the incubator to lay hands on David and pray. I was given permission and laid my hands on my son and prayed. The crying stopped, something had happened. We later learned that the doctor had said that he had seen his first miracle, the nurses in that ward were Christians and had been praying for many years that the doctor would see a miracle.

We had a respite but there were still complications. His brain was functioning well now but his heart wasn't. A specialist was sent from Great Ormond Street hospital to see David. He did not hold out much hope.

We were exhausted, especially Janet, four days of constant prayer. We were in a waiting room, it was dark and gloomy outside. Janet asked me to, in the spirit, look inside David, and see if I could see anything wrong. I looked into David and immediately saw a black beetle moving in his heart. In the spirit I put my sword into David's body and into the beetle, I then pulled both out of him. As this happened the weather broke outside and the sun shined into the room and we cried.

The next tests done on David showed that he was completely healed, we had our perfect baby, that we were able to take home a couple of days later. (As I am writing this I am in tears with the memory. Thank you Jesus for saving my son.)

This, of course, throws up many questions in my mind as to how these spirits procreate.
Most created things are able to procreate, in Genesis 6 we see the sons of God coming down and mating with the daughters of man.

> Now it came to pass, when men began to multiply on the face of the earth, and daughters were born to them, ² that the sons of God saw the daughters of men, that they *were* beautiful; and they took wives for themselves of all whom they chose. ³ And the LORD said, "My Spirit shall not strive with man forever, for he *is* indeed flesh; yet his days shall be one hundred and twenty years." ⁴ There were giants on the earth in those days, and also afterward, when the sons of God came in to the daughters of men and they bore *children* to them. Those *were* the mighty men who *were* of old, men of renown. (Genesis 6:1-4 NKJ)

I wondered whether something had come through our bloodline that was growing in our baby son. There are so many things we do not understand, yet.

Four years later, when my wife was pregnant with our daughter Sophia, I decided I would look into her heart before she was born, so as to prevent later problems.

I was exercising in our local swimming pool when I decided to pray and look into our unborn daughter. As I was swimming I looked, in the spirit, into her heart and saw three tiny black spots, very small. I used my sword to pull each one out. As I reached the end of the pool, a lady in the pool looked directly into my eyes and exclaimed 'well done!' I knew God was talking to me through her, I wondered if she was an angel, or whether she had been prompted to say that. She never said anything else to me.

Chapter 13

Put on the Full Armor of God

For we do not wrestle against flesh and blood, but against principalities, against powers, against the rulers of the darkness of this age, against spiritual *hosts* of wickedness in the heavenly *places.* [13] Therefore take up the whole armor of God, that you may be able to withstand in the evil day, and having done all, to stand. [14] Stand therefore, having girded your waist with truth, having put on the breastplate of righteousness, [15] and having shod your feet with the preparation of the gospel of peace; [16] above all, taking the shield of faith with which you will be able to quench all the fiery darts of the wicked one. [17] And take the helmet of salvation, and the sword of the Spirit, which is the word of God; [18] praying always with all prayer and supplication in the Spirit, being watchful to this end with all perseverance and supplication for all the saints -- Ephesians 6:12-18 NKJV

If the Lord calls you, and He calls many, to fight in the spirit, then it is of the utmost importance that you take the command to 'put on the whole armor of God' seriously.

Reading the scriptures on the armor, does not put on the armor. It only makes you aware of it. We need to understand that this armor is 'real' and not simply a picture.

When King David, as a youth, went to fight the giant Goliath he was offered King Saul's armor to fight with. David turned down the offer as he had not tested King Saul's armor.

> Then Saul clothed David with his garments and put a bronze helmet on his head, and he clothed him with armor. [39] And David girded his sword over his armor and tried to walk, for he had not tested *them*. So David said to Saul, "I cannot go with these, for I have not tested *them*." And David took them off. (1 Samuel 17:38-39 NAS)

Although it may have been embarrassing for David to refuse King Saul's armor it was a matter of life and death. The time to test your armor is not in the battle.

We are going to look at how to put on the armor and also how King David was using his spiritual armor whilst fighting Goliath.

Stand therefore, having girded your waist with truth.. (Ephesians 6:14 NKJV)

The truth is of great importance to our Father. In fact He says, through John, that He has no greater joy than to see his children walking in truth.

I have no greater joy than to hear that my children walk in truth. (3 John 1:4 NKJV)

Jesus says that He is the Truth, (John 14:6), the Holy Spirit is described as 'The Spirit of Truth', (John 15:26), and the Word is described as 'Truth'. (John 17:17)

We see that we are born again by a seed, the word of God, being planted in our body which grows into the new man.

> Having been born again, not of corruptible seed but incorruptible, through the word of God which lives and abides forever, (1 Peter 1:23 NKJV)

The concept that 'truth is sown into people', is important because we need to know the truth, so that if our enemy tries to sow a lie into us, we can refuse it. Also we can sow the truth into others and into the world.

In Strong's concordance, the word translated in the New King James Version as 'waist' and 'loins' in the King James Version, is the Greek **os fuz** (osphus)

From Strong's Concordance.

3751 Οσφυς osphus {os-foos'}
Meaning: 1) the hip (loin) 1a) to gird, gird about, the loins 2) a loin, the (two) loins 2a) the place where the Hebrews thought the generative power (semen) resided

In a spiritual battle a demon may try and sow lies into you, he may say that he is going to destroy you or tell you that you do not have authority to come against him. If you believe, and receive, these words it can destroy your faith to overcome. We must know the truth and not allow lies to grow in us.

As Goliath spoke to the men of Israel, many of them were dreadfully afraid. They had received the words and allowed fear to grow.

As Goliath, the Philistine, came to battle with David, he tried to speak fear into him.

> The Philistine said to David, "Come to me, and I will give your flesh to the birds of the air and the beasts of the field!" 45 Then David said to the Philistine, "You come to me with a sword, with a spear, and with a javelin. But I come to you in the name of the LORD of hosts, the God of the armies of Israel, whom you have defied. 46 "This day the LORD will deliver you into my hand, and I will strike you and take your head from you. And this day I will give the carcasses of the camp of the Philistines to the birds of the air and the wild beasts of the earth, that all the earth may know that there is a God in Israel. 47 "Then all this assembly shall know that the LORD does not save with sword and spear; for the battle *is* the LORD's, and He will give you into our hands." (1 Samuel 17:44-47 NKJV)

What Goliath was saying was not the truth, David spoke the words of truth back to Goliath. Goliath had defied the armies of Israel, and the Lord did deliver him into David's hand.

David was using his armor, he had girt his loins with truth. The truth that David used, wasn't hurriedly put together on the battle field, but had come from his love of the word and truth, spending time with God.

If we tell lies, it will make it a lot harder for us to discern truth. Obey the instruction in Ephesians 4:25 to put away lying.

Preparation for girding our loins with truth, is making sure that any lies we have told are repented of. You don't want to go into battle vulnerable.

Try to see in the spirit, look to see if your loins are girt with truth. Ask the Holy Spirit to expose any lies that have been sown in your heart. Arm yourself with truth, studying the scriptures, so that you can refuse all lies spoken to you through man or unclean spirit.

....having put on the breastplate of righteousness
Ephesians 6:14 NKJV

As Christians we have become the righteousness of God, because we have received the gift of righteousness.

> For He made Him who knew no sin *to be* sin for us, that we might become the righteousness of God in Him. (2 Corinthians 5:21)

> For if by the one man's offense death reigned through the one, much more those who receive abundance of grace and of **the gift of righteousness** will reign in life through the One, Jesus Christ.) (Romans 5:17)

Yet sometimes we are blinded by the revelation of the gift of righteousness, received by faith through grace, that we sometimes forget that we are also called to pursue righteousness.

Timothy, a man of God, was exhorted by Paul to purse righteousness by fleeing from lusts.

> But you, *O man of God,* flee these things and *pursue righteousness,* godliness, faith, love, patience, gentleness. (1 Timothy 6:11 NKJV)

> *Flee also youthful lusts*, but pursue righteousness, faith, love, peace with those who call on the Lord out of a pure heart. (2 Timothy 2:22 NKJV)

Although we have received the gift of righteousness, that is not the end of righteousness. We must flee lusts and continue to purse righteousness.

We have already put on the breastplate of righteousness, but I would recommend trying to see the condition of your breastplate in the spirit. Does it look bright and healthy, or a little tired looking? Lusts and sins can cause weakness in our armor. Ask the Holy Spirit to show any areas of sin or lust that needs repenting of. He is faithful to cleanse us of all unrighteousness when we repent.

> If we confess our sins, He is faithful and just to forgive us *our* sins and to cleanse us from all unrighteousness. (1 John 1:9 NKJV)

Notice how King David was aware of his breastplate. When he spoke to Goliath, he did not come in his own strength and nature but boldly proclaimed—

> For who *is* this uncircumcised Philistine, that he should defy the armies of the living God?" (1 Samuel 17:26)

Goliath, had obviously not received the covenant from Abraham through the token of circumcision. His defiance of God's armies displayed his unrighteousness.

> I come to you *in the name* of the LORD of hosts, the God of the armies of Israel, whom you have defied. (1 Samuel 17:45)

Just as we are the righteousness of God *in* Christ, David was not entering the battle *in* his own
qualities and righteousness but *in the name* of the LORD of hosts. He was wearing his breastplate of righteousness.

and having shod your feet with the preparation of the gospel of peace; (Ephesians 6:15 NKJV)

I was looking at my feet in the spirit one day, and realized that my feet were not properly covered. I could see my toes sticking out. (In the spirit.)

I realized that I was not in peace, my peace had been disturbed.

Thank God, that He always gives us a plan how to deal with things.

Lack of peace generally comes from unbelief, fear or anxieties.

These can be dealt with by casting our cares upon the Lord.

> Therefore humble yourselves under the mighty hand of God, that He may exalt you in due time, [7] casting all your care upon Him, for He cares for you. (1 Peter 5:6-7 NKJV)

We are told that there is nothing that we should be anxious about.

> Be anxious for nothing, but in everything by prayer and supplication, with thanksgiving, let your requests be made known to God; [7] and the peace of God, which surpasses all understanding, will guard your hearts and minds through Christ Jesus. (Philippians 4:6-7 NKJV)

Note that once all of our anxieties have been comprehensively prayed through, with supplications and thanksgiving. THEN we receive a quality of peace which will surpass all understanding of our problems.

Our feet will be shod with the good news of peace. Peace is available.

If we still have fearfulness after going through the above procedures then it may be that we have a spirit of fearfulness. This spirit will stop us operating in love and power. But the good news is that we have a sound mind and can choose to do something about it. We can refuse to be fearful and repent and cast that spirit out. You may need to ask someone to help you with this.

> For God has not given us a spirit of fearfulness, but of power and of love and of a sound mind. (2 Timothy 1:7)

Let us compare how Saul and Israel reacted to the words of Goliath, with David's reaction.

And the Philistine said, "I defy the armies of Israel this day; give me a man, that we may fight together." [11] When Saul and all Israel heard these words of the Philistine, *they were dismayed and greatly afraid.* **1 Samuel 17:10-11** NKJV

Then David said to Saul, "Let no man's heart fail because of him; your servant will go and fight with this Philistine." **1 Samuel 17:32**

King David, although still a youth, was undoubtedly walking in peace with no signs of fear.

David's feet were shod with peace.

Above all, taking the shield of faith with which you will be able to quench all the fiery darts of the wicked one. Ephesians 6:16 NKJV

Again looking in the spirit, what does your shield look like? Keep trying to see, even if you don't see anything, keep trying. Praying in tongues can help you see better, you are stimulating your spirit man, connecting with God in prayer.

When I am praying into my shield, I am not simply believing that I will not get hurt, I am believing that God's word is true —

No weapon formed against you shall prosper, And every tongue *which* rises against you in judgment You shall condemn. *This is the heritage of the servants of the LORD, And their righteousness is from Me,"* Says the LORD. **Isaiah 54:17** NKJV

And we know that all things work together for good to those who love God, to those who are the called according to *His* purpose. **Romans 8:28** NKJV

If you love God, and are called according to His purpose, I hope we all are, then nothing can happen to us that will not outwork in good for us.

When I am engaging in spiritual warfare, I am continually thanking the Lord, that 'No weapon formed against me shall prosper.' My belief that this scripture is true, strengthens my shield of faith.

Even if you do get injured, the process then has to work together for good.

Recently I was engaged in a spiritual battle with four of my friends when I was actually hit by a 'fiery dart'. I was sick for a couple of weeks. The Lord showed one of my friends, not involved with the battle, that an arrow had hit me. He came and pulled it out, in the spirit. The Lord gave him a word for me that He never leaves his wounded without care. I was quite touched that the Lord would have that grace and kindness for his wounded soldiers. Another acquaintance not involved in that battle said that he could see where the wound was, and that it was healing well.

He incidentally pointed to the exact spot where the arrow was pulled out from.

It is also useful to know that sometimes when you are cut in the spirit it feels like severe heart burn. If you feel this even when you are not involved in warfare, immediately ask for the Lord to cover you with his blood, and start praying in the spirit. You may have been struck in the spirit by something/someone.

Using Romans 8:28 is very useful for *all* situations. There is nothing that can work bad for us, unless we give it the power to by believing it is working evil.

One morning I heard noise in our music store, below our apartment. I went to investigate, to find three robbers in the shop. They ran away, but the shop was a complete mess with 1000's of pounds of instruments stolen.

I was in tears, I said to the Lord. "Lord, I know this is going to work together for good. I don't know how it is going to work together for good, but I know that it will do. Lord will you please tell me how it is going to work together for good, though I appreciate that if you don't want to tell me, I will still believe that it is?"

He replied " What did you ask Me to do last week?" Thinking for a moment I replied. " I asked You if you could help me to get rid of all the Yamaha equipment, but Lord all the Alesis equipment has gone too."
Speaking to my wife later about what the Lord had said to me, she responded that she had asked the Lord to help us get rid of the Alesis equipment.

The Yamaha and Alesis equipment had all depreciated a great amount, so that now they were worth at least half of what we had paid for them. But the insurance companies policy was to pay you what you had paid on the invoices for the equipment, not what they were currently worth.

Therefore the Lord had helped us to immediately liquidate our outdated inventory, and receive double what we could have sold it for. This was equivalent to 40,000 dollars and became the deposit on a house we wanted to buy.

I would have still believed the scripture that 'all things work together for good' even if He had not told me how. But He did.

Build yourself up on your most Holy faith, praying in the Holy Spirit.

> But you, beloved, building yourselves up on your most holy faith, praying in the Holy Spirit, (**Jude 1:20** NKJV)

Pray in the spirit until you know that your shield is strong, and then ask the Holy Spirit if you need to continue in prayer.

The devil will try and break down our faith with fear and intimidation.

One day, I had a warlock come into my music store. He said that he wanted to inform me that three witch's covens in the local area were praying against us. Also he said that Satan had asked him to deliver a message to me. The message was that he was going to completely destroy me, and that he had decided that he was going to personally do it.

I paused for a moment and then replied to the warlock, could he pass my reply back to Satan. He said "Yes". I said "could you tell him to talk to Jesus about it."

You see, Jesus is my Lord, and nothing can happen to me that will not work together for good.

King David used his faith when Goliath spoke to him.

Goliath said:

"Come to me, and I will give your flesh to the birds of the air and the beasts of the field!" (1 Samuel 17:44)

Goliath was attempting to describe the future.

David did not receive or believe these words. His shield of faith extinguished these fiery darts, intended to create fear.

David replied with words of faith, a different version of the future, which took place. --

> "You come to me with a sword, with a spear, and with a javelin. But I come to you in the name of the LORD of hosts, the God of the armies of Israel, whom you have defied. 46 "This day the LORD will deliver you into my hand, and I will strike you and take your head from you. And this day I will give the

carcasses of the camp of the Philistines to the birds of the air and the wild beasts of the earth, that all the earth may know that there is a God in Israel. (1 Samuel 17:45-46 NKJV)

King David did not suddenly learn faith, for this time and battle. There had been a preparation, made in his heart.

Father had given him experiences to build his faith.

> But David said to Saul, "Your servant used to keep his father's sheep, and when a lion or a bear came and took a lamb out of the flock, ³⁵ I went out after it and struck it, and delivered *the lamb* from its mouth; and when it arose against me, I caught *it* by its beard, and struck and killed it. ³⁶ "Your servant has killed both lion and bear; and this uncircumcised Philistine will be like one of them, seeing he has defied the armies of the living God." ³⁷ Moreover David said, "The LORD, who delivered me from the paw of the lion and from the paw of the bear, He will deliver me from the hand of this Philistine." (1 Samuel 17:34-37)

Even the father of faith 'Abraham', needed to be strengthened with faith, to receive the promise of Isaac.

> He did not waver at the promise of God through unbelief, *but was strengthened in faith*, giving glory to God, (Romans 4:20 NKJV)

Let us remember to build ourselves up on our Holy faith, praying in the Holy Spirit.

And take the helmet of salvation, and the

**sword of the Spirit, which is the word of God;
(Ephesians 6:17 NKJV)**

It would be quite foolish to go into a battle without wearing your helmet. Here the Lord describes the helmet as a helmet of salvation. This is where we need to have the truth in all areas of salvation, not simply the salvation of our souls. In addition to the salvation of our souls the Lord bought for us, health, peace, prosperity and freedom from curses.

When we attack Satan's kingdom, then you can be sure that he will try to attach you in sickness, fear, poverty and curses.

The Kingdom of heaven comes through violence, and the violent take it by force. Joshua needed to be strong and *very* courageous when he led Israel into the Promised Land.

The following is a list of verses that can be used as part of your helmet of salvation. You need to know your rights and believe the scriptures. This is not meant to be a comprehensive list, but samples of scriptures you will need to fight the wiles of the devil.

The helmet covers our mind, and a lot of the battle is in this realm, where the spirit of the mind is reacting with the Kingdom of heaven.

> (For the weapons of our warfare *are* not carnal, but mighty through God to the pulling down of strong holds;) [5] Casting down imaginations, and every high thing that exalteth itself against the knowledge of God, and *bringing into captivity every thought to the obedience of Christ*; (2 Corinthians 10:4-5 KJV)

Salvation of the soul
A spirit may try to intimidate you by saying you are not saved.

This is nonsense, we know the process of salvation.

> But the righteousness of faith speaks in this way, "Do not say in your heart, 'Who will ascend into heaven?' " (that is, to bring Christ down *from above)* ⁷ or, " 'Who will descend into the abyss?' " (that is, to bring Christ up from the dead). ⁸ But what does it say? "The word is near you, in your mouth and in your heart" (that is, the word of faith which we preach): ⁹ *that if you confess with your mouth the Lord Jesus and believe in your heart that God has raised Him from the dead, you will be saved.* (Romans 10:6-9 NKJV)

Salvation in health and peace

Satan or his minions may attempt to give you a sickness, or try to worry you with anxieties. No thank you, don't receive it.

> But He *was* wounded for our transgressions, *He was* bruised for our iniquities; The chastisement for our peace *was* upon Him, And by His stripes we are healed. (Isaiah 53:5)

> Bless the LORD, O my soul; And all that is within me, *bless* His holy name! ² Bless the LORD, O my soul, And forget not all His benefits: ³ Who forgives all your iniquities, Who heals all your diseases, ⁴ Who redeems your life from destruction, Who crowns you with lovingkindness and tender mercies, ⁵ Who satisfies your mouth with good *things, So that* your youth is renewed like the eagle's. (Psalm 103:1-5)

Salvation from poverty

You may get attacked in your finances. Resist and the devil will flee.

For you know the grace of our Lord Jesus Christ, that though He was rich, yet for your sakes He became poor, that you through His poverty might become rich. (2 Corinthians 8:9)

Beloved, I wish above all things that thou mayest prosper and be in health, even as thy soul prospereth. (3 John 1:2)

Salvation from curses
If something/someone tries to curse you, whether it is legal or not, does not matter. Jesus has paid the price for it on the cross.

Christ hath redeemed us from the curse of the law, being made a curse for us: for it is written, Cursed *is* every one that hangeth on a tree: (Galatians 3:13)

Note how Goliath tries to put Israel under slavery. (The word translated as servants can be translated as slaves.)

Then he stood and cried out to the armies of Israel, and said to them, "Why have you come out to line up for battle? *Am* I not a Philistine, and you the servants of Saul? Choose a man for yourselves, and let him come down to me. ⁹ "If he is able to fight with me and kill me, then we will be your servants. But if I prevail against him and kill him, *then you shall be our servants and serve us.*" (1 Samuel 17:8-9)

King David was not about to become a slave to unrighteousness. He proclaimed.

For who *is* this uncircumcised Philistine, that he should defy the armies of the living God?" (1 Samuel 17:26)

We need to know who we are, and what salvation Jesus has bought for us. This is all contained in the word, and is why it says --

> Take the helmet of salvation, and the sword of the Spirit, *which is the word of God*; (Ephesians 6:17 NKJV)

Take time to look in the spirit at your helmet, what condition is it in, bright and strong or dull and weak? Work at it, know your scriptures, pray in the Holy Spirit.

Now take time to look in the spirit at your sword, what condition is it in, bright and strong or dull and weak?

I was considering if or when King David used his spiritual sword against Goliath.
The answer comes from the translation of the word 'word' in Ephesians 6:17, it is the Greek word 'rhema'.

Definition of rhema by Strongs Concordance
4487 ρημα rhema {hray'-mah}
Meaning: 1) that which is or has been uttered by the living voice, thing spoken, word 1a) any sound produced by the voice and having definite meaning

Looking for a spoken word from God, through David, we find this spoken to Goliath:

> This day will the LORD deliver thee into mine hand; and I will smite thee, and take thine head from thee; and I will give the carcases of the host of the Philistines this day unto the fowls of the air, and to the wild beasts of the earth; that all the earth may know that there is a God in Israel. [47] And all this

assembly shall know that the LORD saveth not with sword and spear: for the battle *is* the LORD'S, and he will give you into our hands. (1 Samuel 17:46-47)

We can see that King David used all of the armor in Ephesians chapter six in his battle with Goliath. These are real weapons and need to be treated with respect.

Chapter 14

Fighting in the Spirit

Before engaging in spiritual warfare, in addition to putting on the full armor of God, it is recommended that one asks Father to cover one with the blood of Jesus. I cannot give you a specific scripture for this, but many experienced Christians in the deliverance field recommend this.

I would also seriously recommend that before fighting a spirit one enquires of God whether it is alright to fight it.

I have already mentioned some of the creatures I have seen in the spirit, beetles and octopus. We will now look at some others.

Giant Spider

Visiting Hampton Court Palace in London, England, I was waiting for my wife sitting in my car in the car lot. I decided that rather than just waste the time waiting, I would look in the spirit and see if I could see the ruling spirit of the palace.

As I was looking I could see a giant spider, it was so huge that it covered the whole of the palace. It was sitting on the roof with big hairy legs reaching to the ground, so it covered the whole of the building.

I asked the Lord if I could go and fight the spirit, he said I could. Using my armor, I went and attacked the spirit, cutting it up with my sword. When my wife, Janet, returned to the car she brought a little booklet from the gift shop. On the inside page of the Hampton Court Palace guide it said that it was forbidden to kill spiders on the grounds of Hampton Court. This law had been in force since the time of King Henry VIII.

Later I found out that the spider I saw in the spirit was a variety of spider only found at Hampton Court and the surrounding area. I was not aware of this when I saw it. It is good to have confirmations of what we are seeing in the spirit.

God of the underworld

I was visiting a house in Bridgend, South Wales, United Kingdom. I was in one of the upstairs rooms when I saw a man standing beside me completely in black. I don't mean dressed in black, simply completely black, pitch black.

'Be gone from here in the name of Jesus' I commanded.
'I won't' he replied, 'I am a god of the underworld and this hill has been given to me'.
Although I believed that he had been given the hill by previous occupants, I did not believe that that had precedent over the authority in the name of Jesus. Remember what we looked at in the last chapter about girding ourselves with truth. The truth is that all authority has been given to Jesus in heaven and earth.

That spirit thought that he would win by arguing a case that did not bear scrutiny.

> And Jesus came and spoke to them, saying, "All authority has been given to Me in heaven and on earth. (Matthew 28:18 NKJV)

I replied to him 'I don't care, all authority has been given to Jesus, and I command you to leave this property and not return in the name of Jesus'. The spirit left.

The next day, it was quite noticeable that all the birds from the local area were now sitting on the property that had been cleansed. Perhaps they were aware of the freedom.

Female Deity

In 2008 I was living in Chislehurst, Kent, in the suburbs of South East London. We noticed that there was a disturbing amount of reports of cancer and other related problems, especially in the churches and ministers wives. Some were dying. It did not seem to be normal. In prayer the Holy Spirit revealed to my wife, Janet, that the outbreak was being orchestrated by a female deity that was situated in the caves under the area. I asked the Lord if I was to fight it, and He said yes.

I spent approximately three weeks praying and fighting in the spirit. One day, as I was praying in my car, I felt a break in the spirit. I knew that the female deity had been defeated. Suddenly the Lord spoke to me.

'Martin, I want you now to believe for the spoils of war.'

This was new to me, I had never heard or read about being able to receive spoils of war when a territorial spirit was defeated.

I thought about, whether there was any scriptual reference to this. The closest I could think of was when David received the spoils in 1 Samuel Chapter 30. The Amalekites had raided across the land of Judah and the land of the Philistines. They made the mistake of attacking Ziklag, where David was based from. David recovered all of his own goods and received so much spoil that he was able to send it to the elders of many cities.

> Now when David came to Ziklag, he sent *some* of the spoil to the elders of Judah, to his friends, saying, "Here is a present for you from the spoil of the enemies of the LORD" -- ²⁷ to *those* who *were* in Bethel, *those* who *were* in Ramoth of the South, *those* who *were* in Jattir, ²⁸ *those* who *were* in Aroer, *those* who *were* in Siphmoth, *those* who *were* in Eshtemoa, ²⁹ *those* who *were* in Rachal, *those* who *were* in the cities of the Jerahmeelites, *those* who *were* in the cities of the Kenites, ³⁰ *those* who *were* in Hormah, *those* who *were* in Chorashan, *those* who *were* in Athach, ³¹ *those* who *were* in Hebron, and to all the places where David himself and his men were accustomed to rove. (1 Samuel 30:26-31 NKJV)

The Lord had told me now to believe for the spoils of war. This was amazing because the area of Chislehurst, is an affluent area of London, where many of the bankers from the City of London live.

I continued driving to my home, I was about a minute away. As I walked through the door Janet said –

'Martin, the Lord has just said to me that He wants you to believe for the spoils of war'.
Well that was a quick confirmation, I had not even said a word, she did not know that the spirit had just been defeated, and we

were not aware that one could receive spoils of war.

Beetles entering the Church

In 2009 I was visiting MorningStar ministries in South Carolina, USA. I had been attending some meetings of the Investing with Insight group. They are a body of Christians that invest in the stock markets according to dreams and visions. I love the idea. Their website is www.investingwithinsight.com

It was time for me to catch a plane back to England. I heard a very quiet voice telling me to go back into the main MorningStar auditorium. The voice was so quiet that I felt I could ignore it and go to the airport, I really didn't want to go back in.

Then I was feeling that feeling, the one that makes you feel bad, the feeling that one is letting the Lord down. I couldn't ignore it, even though it had been very quiet. I went back into the auditorium.

"Why am I here", I asked the Lord.
"Look and see what you can see", He replied.

I looked around but could see nothing.
"I can't see anything".
"Keep looking" He replied.

I thought I would go above the building, in the spirit, and see if I could see anything from there.
To my disgust, I could see a swarm of beetles filling up an air vent and trying to enter the church.
I quickly dispatched them with my sword. The vent was now clear and clean.
Returning to my car, I felt the joy of the Lord, mission accomplished.

The next time I returned to MorningStar, just over a year later, I looked in the spirit to see if the beetles had returned, but the vent was still clean.

Working from my bed

Over the years, I have developed the habit of fighting spirits from my bed. If I can't sleep I ask
the Lord, if I can go and fight something. It makes for some exciting stories, fighting dragons etc..

My full name is Martin Dominic Powell.

Martin means *Man of war*
Dominic means *Of the LORD* In Latin
Powell means *Son of the servant of St. Paul* In Gaelic

My family name comes from the Gaelic Mac Giolla Phoil, which was later anglicized to Powell

My mother told me that God had given her my name, so I was born to fight.

I have found that you don't need to be in the same location of a spirit to be able to fight it.
Somehow you can just 'be there'. This is NOT astral projecting, which is when your whole soul comes out of the body. I think it is similar to when Paul was speaking to the Corinthians in regards to judging the man that had sexual immorality with his father's wife.

> For I indeed, as *absent in body but present in spirit*, have already judged (as though I were present) him who has so done this deed. ⁴ In the name of our

Lord Jesus Christ, when you are gathered together, *along with my spirit*, with the power of our Lord Jesus Christ deliver such a one to Satan for the destruction of the flesh, that his spirit may be saved in the day of the Lord Jesus. (1 Corinthians 5:3-5 NKJV)

Paul was absent in body but present in spirit. The instruction to deliver the man over to Satan, for the destruction of his flesh, was to be done, whilst Paul's spirit was with them. This is an unusual portion of scripture, but I have found that one can fight in the spirit from another location.

In approximately 2009/2010 I was asking the Lord if I could fight, from London, a spirit of leviathan, that I had heard was causing trouble for MorningStar ministries. The Lord said 'no' to me. This was the first time He had ever said that I could not fight a spirit. Not being completely sure of the word, and perhaps never having heard that I was not to fight a spirit. I gave the leviathan spirit a quick whack with my sword. Immediately I felt struck across my chest and head, it was quite severe pain. I obviously realized that it was the Lord who said 'no', and quickly repented. I would have to wait until 2011 before the Lord would give me a plan to attack this leviathan.

Chapter 15

USA and MorningStar

I love America and Americans. I expect this goes back to the fact that, as a prodigal son, I gave my whole life back to the Lord under the American ministry 'Maranatha'. There was so much love and fellowship in that ministry. Subconsciously, and consciously, I must associate love and warmness with Americans and American accents.

As a young Christian in 1983 the Lord told me that I would not be going to America straight away but that it would be later. Nearly every year from 1983 to 2010 the Lord would tell me that I was going to America. 'Martin you're going to America', 'Martin you're going to America', 'Martin you're going to America', 'Martin you're going to America'. All the time I would hear this.

Also I was given a detailed word from a lady in London listing all the American cities that I would be ministering in.

In 2007 I said to the Lord, 'Lord you keep saying I'm going to America, open up a way and I will go.'

David Shadbolt, a prophet and a friend, was ministering at my church 'The New Haven Fellowship'. 'Martin', he said, 'I really feel that the Lord wants you to check out MorningStar ministries'.

I followed this leading, and attended the MorningStar worship and warfare conference in 2007.
It was my first trip to the USA, and I loved it. It was as if I had come home. To my astonishment Bob Weiner, the founder of Maranatha, was on the board of MorningStar. Of all the churches in America, over 300,000, the man whose ministry had led me to the Lord, was part of the church I was led to come over 'the pond' to see. This was an amazing probability.

I was connected with Christian Pastors, Christian Businessmen, Christian Musicians, Christians in the arts, a Christian school, Christian teachers and Christian friends. I thought I had come to the 'New Jerusalem', (and I haven't changed my mind 6 years later as I write this.)

I knew that it was time now to move over to America. After the two week trip, I returned to London. Sitting next to me in my car a friend, who knew nothing of my thoughts, turned and said to me 'Martin, you are an American'. I replied 'yes, but you can't tell from my accent.'

The Lord, then started saying to me 'Martin I am making you an American, of the highest order.'
This word was repeated to me for the next three years, as we struggled to get our visas.

I knew that we needed to get Green Cards, permanent residence.

This was going to be a major move, we would need to sell our house, our business and find work in America. I didn't want, with two young children, the stress of having to renew visas every two years or so, with all the lawyers, expense and uncertainty that it would cause.

The journey to get the green cards started in December 2007. Janet, my wife, was happy that we were on the right track and I went to visit lawyers in London. We spent a lot of money with them, taking over a year and they failed to get the green card.

This was quite a setback, but we carried on believing that we were coming to America. The Lord had already previously used me to help two couples move from one continent to another, with all the visa complications, and had given me faith to help them. Now I was having to use that faith for my own family. The Lord carried on telling me that we were going to America, faith comes by hearing, so I continued.

I was introduced to Jorge Parrott, by Rose Jarboe. Rose is a lovely woman, whom I had met at MorningStar, she was obviously an anointed woman of God. She prayed with great gusto that we would be able to come to America and connected me with Jorge, who is the president of CMM, Christ's Mandate for Missions, the missionary arm of MorningStar ministries.

Jorge is one of those meek, great, men of God. Overseeing a tremendous amount of works for the Lord, he moves simply in the flow of the Spirit. He offered me employment as a Pastor at CMM, helping me to transition to the USA.

Gwen Cattron, handled the visas for CMM. After 9/11 religious visas became much harder to obtain. Gwen skillfully negotiated the new regulations to bring us the much sought after 'Green Cards' we had all been praying for. We quickly became friends, speaking almost daily for many months regarding the visa. We found we shared a love for the word of God. She is a hidden treasure.

On the 2nd of November 2010 Janet and I were in the US Embassy in London, receiving our final interview before acceptance for permanent residence.

It was a stressful climax to three years of planning, paperwork, and preparation.
Tears of joy followed the announcement that we had been accepted. On arriving home, at my mother's house, I immediately booked the airline tickets for the 16th of November in two weeks time. My mother was probably as relieved as we were, she had kindly put us up in her home since March 2010. We had sold our home in expectancy of emigrating.

A new chapter of our lives was about to begin.

Chapter 16

Part II of My Life
Living in the New World

We arrived at Charlotte Douglas International Airport on the evening of the 16th of November 2010, it was now the 17th of November back in London, 5 hours ahead. I was born on the 17th November 1962 in London, so I had completed exactly 48 years living as a British man in England. The rest of my life to be an American, based in America.

Before leaving England the Lord had said to me that He had a surprise for me. I asked him what it was?
You can guess the answer. He said it wouldn't be a surprise if he told me. I smiled.

The spiritual climate in America was noticeably different. In London, I would worship the Lord on my keyboard, after around twenty to thirty minutes, I would notice the presence of the Lord. In Fort Mill, South Carolina, I would feel the presence of the Lord almost before I played a note. What a wonderful country to live in.

Soon after moving to America, the Lord started bringing people to pray for us. One particular lady was Norma Aguilar. We met in a prayer meeting in Moravian Falls. I had just seen a vision of a chariot of fire, with an angel. Norma, a stranger came up to me and said that the Lord had given to her a mandate to pray and intercede for me. She then related a vision she had seen, which was quite accurate. Norma has said that she prays for me two hours each day.

The Lord then resurrected my clarinet playing. I had been invited to speak on an apostolic round table in Newcastle, Pennsylvania. I was quite happy to talk, but one of the ladies praying for me said that she felt the Lord wanted me to bring my clarinet. As I had not practiced my clarinet seriously for twenty eight years, I did not think it was a good idea. Then another lady rang me on the phone and said that the Lord had told her at 3.30am that I was to take the clarinet. As it was being confirmed I thought that it could be the Lord. I packed the clarinet and Gwen Cattron emailed the organizers of the conference that they should ask me to play, that I had won many competitions in my early years.

At the conference I was asked to play, and I played the slow movement of the Mozart clarinet concerto. Before playing I remembered the word I was given, before laying the clarinet down, that God would start to heal people as I played. I asked for the angels to go among the people and bring healings. I asked for those that felt heat going into their bodies to let me know afterwards. Two people came up to me afterwards and told me that they had been instantly healed

Since then, I have played another fourteen times, with healings being reported most times.
We have had healings of; scoliosis, cancer, depression, injures from a motorbike accident, walking difficulties, bone problems, emotional inner healings, kidney stone disappearing.. etc.. Some

experienced heat in their bodies as they were healed.

I love working for God, and it was nearly time for my 'surprise' that God had promised me in London.

Jorge Parrott asked me to prepare a resume for Rick Joyner, the leader of MorningStar. Instead of writing a resume, based on my musical achievements and church building, I decided to write about my sword fighting experiences in the spirit.

The resume was emailed on the Saturday, and on the Sunday Rick preached on the Knights of the Order of St. John.

The full title is:--

Knights Hospitallers of the Sovereign Order of Saint John of Jerusalem, Knights of Malta - The Ecumenical Order

This is where the word 'hospital' comes from. This order of knights set up the first hospital, in Jerusalem in the 11th Century. The purpose was to provide care and protection to Christian pilgrims to the Holy Land.

Rick Joyner said in his preaching, that he has not taken so much flack over anything in his life as much as joining this order. Yet-- Jesus made it quite clear to him that he was to join.

I expect that Jesus' enemies do not like an order that vows to serve Jesus and the poor. Many of the misguided attacks are through ignorance and unfounded assumptions.

After the service Jorge Parrott and Bill NeSmith, invited me to apply to be a Knight.
I already knew, listening to Rick, and my experiences fighting in the spirit, that I was born to be a Knight. I readily filled in my

application and waited to hear whether it was successful.

I was invested as a Knight on the 22nd January 2010 in Fort Mill, South Carolina. It was a very spiritual experience. The presence of the Holy Spirit was very strong. There were many Knights in attendance, from all around the world. Among them was Prince Anton Esterhazy, I recognized his name from my music history lessons at school. So I boldly asked him if his family had sponsored the composer Haydn, he replied in the affirmative and told me that they have a Haydn festival once a year held in a palace in Hungary. It was good to see so many people standing up for Christ and the poor.

This all happened so quickly after arriving in America, we had only arrived two months previously. One evening I said to my wife, Janet where on earth did this come from. It was a complete 'surprise', and then I laughed remembering what the Lord had said to me in England before we left -- That he had a surprise for me.

After the investiture, I was walking up 'Main Street' in the Heritage International Ministries building, (where MorningStar is based, previously where PTL was.) I clearly heard a voice which said 'Take six Knights and kill it'. I knew it was referring to killing the leviathan spirit.

Chapter 17

Killing Leviathan

B e strong in the Lord and in the power of His might. [11] Put on the whole armor of God, that you may be able to stand against the wiles of the devil. [12] For we do not wrestle against flesh and blood, but *against principalities*, against powers, against the rulers of the darkness of this age, against spiritual *hosts* of wickedness in the heavenly *places*. (Ephesians 6:10-12 NKJV)

Some would say that we should not fight principalities.
The word of God, above, says that we should be strong, and that *we do* wrestle against principalities. Of course this should not be taken lightly.

In that day the LORD with His severe sword, great and strong, Will punish Leviathan the fleeing serpent,

Leviathan that twisted serpent; And He will *slay the reptile* that *is* in the sea. **(Isaiah 27:1** NKJV)

Some would say that one can't kill a spirit.
The word of God says that His Sword, *can slay* the reptile leviathan.

I do not think that it is by chance that legends talk of the Knights killing the dragons. The Knight St. George killed the dragon in England, and England propagated the gospel for centuries, sending missionaries around the world.

Also when talking about spirits we must not make the assumption that there is only one.
When Jesus was speaking about the 'deaf and dumb' spirit in Mark 9:25-29, He said that 'this kind' can come out by nothing but prayer and fasting.

Jesus described this type of spirit after its 'kind'. Creatures multiply after their kind.

'Take six Knights and kill it' (Making seven Knights in total.)

Faith comes by hearing, and hearing by the rhema word of God.
Well -- I had a 'rhema' word.
I asked the Lord for a plan.

'Go to Moravian Falls, and fight it over a weekend.'
I now had a second rhema word.

I am not going to write an in depth analysis of leviathan here, simply narrating testimony.
However this spirit manifests it's character in many ways, division between brethren, arrogance, twisting words, pride etc..

I submitted the plan to Bill NeSmith and Jorge Parrott, and in agreement the plan was then submitted to Rick Joyner. To be fair Rick was neither for nor against the fight, but most importantly gave us permission to go ahead. Without that permission it would have been impossible to fight the spirit. The very nature of that spirit is to cause division.

Next the plan was communicated to all the knights in the Carolinas, those that were interested were to come to a meeting.

In the meeting the sobriety of the task was discussed. See Job chapter 41 and Isaiah 27:1.

Each knight who took part in the battle needed to know that it was possible that they would not come back. That they may die. How many apostles and saints have died for the cause?

Even with that knowledge more knights than were needed volunteered.

Preparations were made, a date was chosen, Bill NeSmith called a 21 day fast and studies of our enemy and studies of the armor of God were made.

Before each phase of the battle, we broke bread, making sure that we were clean. The battle was hard but not as tough as I thought it would be. The Lord later told me that this particular leviathan was old, and that the next one we would fight was younger, and would be harder.

We asked that all the intercessors involved would only pray in support of the knights taking part, we did not want anyone not in the room to attack the spirit and be vulnerable.

After we had cut the head off the leviathan we received a text from one of the intercessors who said that they had just seen in the spirit the head being cut off. We also saw the belly of this creature ripped open with our swords, out of the belly came gold coins, buildings, and ministries set free. We also saw a silver collar that was around the neck of the creature, with chains leading from it to people. It is interesting, in legend, that dragons sit guarding the treasure.

We are quite aware, that when you are fighting in the invisible, it is sometimes hard to confirm what you are achieving. We asked the Lord to bring confirmations to us from sources that would not be aware of the battle.

The confirmations started to come in immediately.

The Sunday Rick Joyner announced that property, worth millions, had been given to MorningStar.

On the Monday, a lady at an intercession meeting at MorningStar related that she had a dream over the weekend where she saw a great sea creature have it's head cut off, and that living waters were then released.

On the Monday, Jorge Parrot received a phone call donating 185,000 dollars to CMM.

He also received that day a recording of intercessors, unaware of the battle, interceding for Jorge proclaiming 'no weapon formed against you shall prosper'. The scripture we were using for our shields of faith.

There were many more confirmations.

Are we now free from all the works of that principality?
I don't think so.

Leviathan is the head over many lesser spirits, pride, lies, deception, fraud, arrogance etc..

Each of these spirits that have manifested through the flesh of the people need to be cast out, through repentance and the cleansing of the blood of Jesus. But the major force that was driving these spirits has been dealt with.

Now for the next battle.

Chapter 18

Kingdom Talents

"I can see the word 'Mint' written on you" I was receiving the first prophetic ministry I had had at Morningstar ministries. I filed it away in the back of my mind, with other prophecies that were interesting, but which I did not know what they meant.

Having arrived in America without a job, I had been earnestly asking the Lord what He wanted me to do.

"Martin, I want you to make money", this was not the first time that God had replied to me that He wanted me to make money.

I had moved to the USA from England in the Autumn of 2010, when I left London the Lord had told me that He wanted me to be his banker. I did not know what that meant.

Attending the KEYS conference, Kingdom Economic Yearly

Summit, in MorningStar in 2011, again I asked the Lord what He wanted me to do.

"Martin, I want you to make money"

Finally the penny dropped, it wasn't that the Lord wanted me to make money, in the business sense, but that He wanted me to manufacture money. The word money in the old testament literally means silver. So we started the process to manufacture silver rounds called 'Talents'.

These are silver bullion rounds, and therefore cannot be called coins, which is reserved for legal tender.

Incredibly, we found out later that the word Talent in Hebrew literally means 'round', the legal designation!!! I danced around my office when I discovered this.

[Disclaimer: Please note that we do not manufacture our Silver and Gold Talents as a currency. They are simply Gold and Silver bullion rounds that have their value in the precious metal they contain.]

A short while later, I was on a mountain in North Carolina, called prayer mountain in Moravian Falls. A minister from South Africa, Erni Visser, told me that the Lord had told him that there was to be a new economy on the earth based on the Talent.

I was extremely surprised as he did not know that we were the ones called to manufacture them, and that we had already started the process!

He came from Africa and I came from Europe, meeting in the USA, and he was confirming my assignment from the Lord Jesus.

The designs for the Talents took between 6-8 weeks and were put together by my wife Janet, she had majored in design for 8 years, and received from the Lord the design He wanted.

We have now minted hundreds of thousands, soon to be millions, of the Silver Talents and they are flying all over the world.

We have seen many people crying when looking at the beautiful Silver Talents. I asked one lady why she was crying, and she said "because God is doing something". She was aware that the Lord was coming back and we were preparing for the transition for His Government to be set up on Earth.

The Lord also instructed me to put His name on each of the Talents. Hidden in the left wing in Hebrew script is the word "Yeshua" יֵשׁוּעַ

"Thy name is ointment poured forth" (Song of Solomon 1:3). Each Silver Talent carries the beauty and anointing of Jesus' name.

Details of the design features of the Silver Talent can be found at the following web page:
https://kingdom-talents.com/talents/silver-talent/

After making the Silver Talents, the Lord then instructed us to now make Gold Talents. The design work came through a lot quicker than the Silver Talent. Again, it was my wife Janet who designed them. This time we made a 1 troy oz version and a 1/10 oz version.

Straight away we knew that the Gold Talent would have the Lion of Judah on the front. I was very excited and awed at what it would look like. Instead of the Hebrew script for Yeshua, used on the Silver Talents, the Gold Talent has the Hebrew script for the word YHWH, יהוה, under the Lion's left ear, (right ear when we look at it.)

On the reverse of the Gold Talent it has, like the Silver Talent, the map of the world, referring to the scripture Rev 11:15

> "The kingdoms of this world are become the Kingdoms of our Lord, and of his Christ; and He shall reign for ever and ever." (Rev 11:15)

The top half of the reverse has a meandering river flowing in to the sea.

> "For the earth shall be filled with the knowledge of the glory of the LORD, as the waters cover the sea." (Hab 2:14)

On the Silver Talent across the center of the reverse it has the words 'lift up your eyes'. This is an encouragement to lift our eyes to God, to also see the promises to Abraham have been fulfilled, to gaze into the heavens for the sign of the Lords return. To see that the House of the Lord is on the highest mountain.

Janet asked me what were the words to go across the center of the Gold Talent. I replied, "God will tell us." She kept asking me for about 3 months. Each time I would reply that God will tell us.

One day we were sitting in the kitchen and again Janet asked me if I had heard yet from the Lord about the words. On the reverse of the Gold Talent there is also the rising sun with rays shining on the river and ocean.

Suddenly, the Lord said to me, 'The Light of the World'. Both myself and my wife started crying at the revelation that

He was the light of the world and was coming back to take His place.

When we started our business "Kingdom Talents – Gold and Silver investments", 2012, it was founded on Rev 3:18 NKJ

> "I counsel you to buy from Me gold refined in the fire, that you may be rich". (Rev 3:18 NKJ)

I had been reading this verse in Revelation, but I could not understand how to buy gold from God. As I meditated on the verse and asked the Holy Spirit to help me understand it, I decided to look up the words in the Greek.

I found that the word 'to buy' in Greek was 'agoradzo'.

It's first meaning in strong's dictionary is 'to be in the market place'

59 αγοραζω agorazo {ag-or-ad'-zo}
Meaning: 1) to be in the market place, to attend it 2) to do business there, buy or sell 3) of idle people: to haunt the market place, lounge there

Straight away I thought 'I can do this'.

In Proverbs it say that he who has pity on the poor LENDS to the Lord, And He will pay back what he has given. (Pro 19:17 NKJ)

Because the Lord has promised to give to us what we have given to the poor then gold would be given to us out of heaven from Jesus, if we give gold to the poor.

Having a plan what to do, I asked the Lord where to give gold. He showed me clearly where to give it.

One lady, Freddie Powers, who has a ministry to the homeless, and an orphanage, was already expecting the gold. God had told her that he was sending her gold.

After giving out the gold, I received the business 'Kingdom Talents - Gold and Silver investments'.

Remarkably during Christmas 2015 I was again giving a Gold Talent to Freddie Powers, the lady who has the orphanage. As I gave it to her, I noticed gold dust all over my trousers, my shirt, and my tie. Freddie then told me that there was gold on my face and it was also found in my ears!

I knew that we had received our business through giving gold to the poor, but I hadn't realized that we would also receive it straight out of heaven!

Details of the design features of the Gold Talents can be found at the following web page:

https://kingdom-talents.com/talents/gold-talent/

Chapter 19

How to Become
One of Jesus' Sheep

This chapter is for those who have not yet given their lives
to Jesus.

One of the problems with listening to spiritual voices, is that
there are many voices to hear.

> My sheep hear my voice, and I know them, and they
> follow me: [28] And I give unto them eternal life; and
> they shall never perish... (John 10:27-28)

> And when he putteth forth his own sheep, he goeth
> before them, and the sheep follow him: *for they know
> his voice.* [5] And a stranger will they not follow, but
> will flee from him: for they know not the voice of
> strangers. (John 10:4-5)

It is reassuring to know that we will hear His voice, we will know

His voice, that we follow Him and not the voice of strangers. Not forgetting --never perishing, and having eternal life!

But these promises are only for His sheep, so how do we become one of the sheep of the great shepherd Jesus?

The bad news is that the wages of sin is death.

The good news is that in Jesus is mercy and grace, and that we can receive the forgiveness of sins and therefore the gift of eternal life.

> For the wages of sin *is* death; but *the gift of God is eternal life* through Jesus Christ our Lord. (Romans 6:23-7:1)

We also learn from the book of Romans, chapter 10, that it is not our job to say who is going to go to heaven, and who is going to go to hell. That's Jesus' job.

But it does say, what we can say.

> But the righteousness of faith speaks in this way, "Do not say in your heart, 'Who will ascend into heaven?' " (that is, to bring Christ down *from above)* [7] or, " 'Who will descend into the abyss?' " (that is, to bring Christ up from the dead). [8] *But what does it say?* "The word is near you, in your mouth and in your heart" (that is, the word of faith which we preach): [9] that *if you confess with your mouth the Lord Jesus and believe in your heart that God has raised Him from the dead, you will be saved.* [10] For with the heart one believes unto righteousness, and with the mouth confession is made unto salvation. [11] For the Scripture says, "Whoever believes on Him will not

be put to shame." (Romans 10:6-11 NKJV)

To be saved we need to do two things.
1. Confess with our mouths that Jesus is our Lord.
2. Believe in our hearts that God has raised Jesus from the dead.

Simply saying out loud 'Jesus is my Lord', is not enough. It is the actual act of giving your life to Jesus, so that He 'is your Lord', that is required by the confession. E.g. simply saying 'I do', does not make you married. It is a solemn vow that is needed.

Therefore a solemn prayer is needed in which we give Jesus our lives. He covers our sins with his blood, that is he pays the 'death' required by our sins, and in return we give our lives to Him, under His care, and He now becomes our Lord.

This prayer must not be taken lightly, as it does mean that we are promising to do whatever He asks, and then He, in turn, pays the legal price for sin, on our behalf, and gives us the gift of eternal life.

I would point out here, that I have worked for Jesus all my working life, and there is no one better to serve. Father God created us, he knew all the things we would like, and put those desires into our hearts. Then when we choose to obey Him, we end up doing all the things that He created us for -- complete fulfillment.

Before we can take that step of giving our lives to Jesus, through a solemn prayer, we must look at the second thing that is required. -- Believe in our hearts that God has raised Jesus from the dead.

The faith, belief, that Jesus was raised from the dead, can only come from Heaven. It is the same, as when Peter received faith that Jesus was the son of God.

When Jesus came into the region of Caesarea Philippi, He asked His disciples, saying, "Who do men say that I, the Son of Man, am?" [14] So they said, "Some *say* John the Baptist, some Elijah, and others Jeremiah or one of the prophets." [15] He said to them, "But who do you say that I am?" [16] Simon Peter answered and said, *"You are the Christ, the Son of the living God."* [17] Jesus answered and said to him, "Blessed are you, Simon Bar-Jonah, for *flesh and blood has not revealed this to you, but My Father who is in heaven.* [18] "And I also say to you that you are Peter, and on this rock I will build My church, and the gates of Hades shall not prevail against it. (Matthew 16:13-18 NKJV)

Remember that we are required to believe that Jesus was raised from the dead in our hearts, not in our minds. Our minds, may try and throw up arguments, but faith is in the heart. Look into your own heart and consider, do I believe that Jesus was raised from the dead.

If you do believe then you are ready to move on to a prayer that will place you in the fold of the great Shepherd Jesus, and cause you to be adopted as sons and daughters to the Father of all creation, Almighty God.

If you do not *yet* believe then remember that we do not need to understand, but simply believe.

Trust in the LORD with all your heart, And lean not on your own understanding; [6] In all your ways acknowledge Him, And He shall direct your paths. (Proverbs 3:5-6 NKJV)

Ask and seek God for the faith, it will come.

Ask, and it will be given to you; seek, and you will find; knock, and it will be opened to you. [8] "For everyone who asks receives, and he who seeks finds, and to him who knocks it will be opened. [9] "Or what man is there among you who, if his son asks for bread, will give him a stone? [10] "Or if he asks for a fish, will he give him a serpent? [11] "If you then, being evil, know how to give good gifts to your children, how much more will your Father who is in heaven give good things to those who ask Him! (Matthew 7:7-11 NKJV)

If you are ready to pray the prayer of salvation then take some time to read the prayer through carefully, like a contract, and then you may solemnly pray the prayer out aloud, the angels will be your witnesses.

There are only two requirements of the prayer, which we have just looked at, but often a little 'padding' is put into the prayer. I will give you the scripture references as to why they are included.

Prayer of Salvation

Dear Father, who art in heaven, thank you that you would consider adopting me. (Gal 4:5) I am sorry that I have so far lived a life for myself, selfishly, and not for you. I solemnly ask that you would forgive me of all the sins that I have committed, I do repent, please cleanse me that I may live my life for you righteously. (Acts 3:19, 1 John 1:9)

I do believe that Jesus died on the cross for me, that I may live, and that He was raised from the dead on the third day. I give my life to you Jesus, unreservedly, I will obey You and follow You all the days of my life, You are now my Lord. (Romans 10:6-11, Luke 24:5-7)

Dear Father I ask that the incorruptible seed, the word of God, would come and take root in my heart, causing me to be born again. (1 Peter 1:23)

Finally, Father I ask that You, Jesus and the Holy Spirit would come and dwell in my heart. I ask for these things in the name of Jesus. (John 14:16-23)

But when the fullness of the time had come, God sent forth His Son, born of a woman, born under the law, 5 to redeem those who were under the law, that we might receive the adoption as sons. 6 And because you are sons, God has sent forth the Spirit of His Son into your hearts, crying out, "Abba, Father!" 7 Therefore you are no longer a slave but a son, and if a son, then an heir of God through Christ. (Galatians 4:4-7 NKJV)

"Repent therefore and be converted, that your sins may be blotted out, so that times of refreshing may come from the presence of the Lord, (**Acts 3:19** NKJV)

If we confess our sins, He is faithful and just to forgive us *our* sins and to cleanse us from all unrighteousness. **(1 John 1:9 NKJV)**

… Why seek ye the living among the dead? 6 He is not here, but is risen: remember how he spake unto you when he was yet in Galilee, ⁷ Saying, The Son of man must be delivered into the hands of sinful men, and be crucified, and the third day rise again. (**Luke 24:5-7**)

Being born again, not of corruptible seed, but of incorruptible, by the word of God, which liveth and abideth for ever. (**1 Peter 1:23**)

Jesus answered and said unto him, If a man love me, he will keep my words: and my Father will love him, and we will come unto him, and make *our abode with him*. (**John 14:23**)

And I will pray the Father, and he shall give you another Comforter, that he may abide with you for ever; ¹⁷ *Even* the Spirit of truth; whom the world cannot receive, because it seeth him not, neither knoweth him: but ye know him; for he dwelleth with you, and shall be in you. (**John 14:16-17**)

Now that you have prayed the prayer of salvation, you are born again and have been adopted by our Father in Heaven. The next steps for you will be finding a church that will baptize you in water and the Holy Spirit and that will provide discipleship for you, feeding you with the word of God.

There is only one church, one body, one Spirit. Prayerfully ask the Holy Spirit to lead you to the church that Jesus wants you to attend.

Chapter 20

Introduction to Exercises Listening to the Voice

It is interesting how God inspires us to create. When I am writing a song or speaking or writing, there is always structure. I wanted to write exercises for this book for those who want to practice listening to God. As I was thinking upon them, the Lord showed me that there was to be seven exercises, I knew there were to be seven but didn't know what they were to be about!

Then I realized that there was to be one attached to each day of the week.

As I was pondering why and how I could write an exercise for each day of the week, it came to my mind how I had already written on the seven major parts to a soul's life. Each day was to concentrate on one of these important areas.

After a few years of being a Pastor, I realized that most problems in a person's life could be avoided simply by 'balance'. It reminded me of a circus act, where plates are spun on top of sticks. Whilst the sticks are gyrated the plates spin and don't fall. As more sticks and plates are added the risk of a fall becomes greater, as the performer cannot attend to all of the sticks at once.

It seemed to me that people's lives were being destroyed through imbalance, too much attention being paid to one area, and too little to another. This imbalance could also be observed in families, businesses, churches and ministries, in fact any organism.

Great ministries, bringing multitudes of souls to the Lord, could fall through imbalance.

As I was pondering these things, the obvious areas were coming to my mind, like 'righteousness', 'work' etc..

I asked the Lord how many areas there were. He immediately replied 'seven'. I asked Him, as it was an obvious number, if He would confirm it to me in His Word. Instantly the Lord said to me 'Turn to Proverbs Chapter 9 verse 1'.

I like hearing this way, because it is either going to be spectacularly wrong, or correct.

So I turned to the verse:

> Wisdom has built her house, She has hewn out her seven pillars; (Proverbs 9:1 NKJV)

Well, that verse didn't leave any ambiguity, seven it was. Not only was it seven but it was wisdom to hew out the seven pillars, to support the house. We need to pay attention to these seven pillars.

I asked the Lord what the seven pillars are and what came to mind were the following:

Pillar 1   Seek first the Kingdom of God

Pillar 2   Righteousness/Holiness

Pillar 3   Daily Work – Your Job

Pillar 4   Health

Pillar 5   Money

Pillar 6   Family

Pillar 7   Leisure and Rest

Many of these pillars function together, e.g. our job may be to earn money. Our leisure time, may include time with our family and need money for the activities. Some peoples job will be working for the church, which provides money and health care for their families.

It can sometimes be easy to spot imbalance in ourselves and others:

The business man, who puts so much time into his job and money, that he sacrifices the relationship with his wife and children.

Pastors who spend so much time for the Kingdom, yet lose their children through lack of time spent with them. (Working for God can be costly, don't let Satan fool you into imbalance.)

The evangelist, who ignores money, and spends all his time working for the Kingdom of God.
The lack of money causes cracks in his house, and stress on his family.

The person who treasures time with his family, over time at work. They all suffer from poor quality of life, lack of money and healthcare.

Big ministries have fallen, through not keeping an eye on righteousness. Too much time going into the ministry, too much time spent alone with female assistants. Relationships start to form.
The sincere work for God fails to sin. The reverberations of a big ministry falling, spreads to the ends of the earth.

In the exercises we will be focusing on--asking God questions.
It seems that in many instances God is waiting for us to 'ask'.
He already knows what we need, but he requires us to ask Him. James goes as far as to say that we don't receive because we don't ask.

> ...Your Father knows the things you have need of before you ask Him. (Matthew 6:8 NKJV)

> ... Yet you do not have because you do not ask. (James 4:2 NKJV)

I suggest that each exercise you do once a day, during your time of prayer, and after having prayed through the 'Lords prayer'.

There are many opportunities during the Lord's prayer to ask questions.

"In this manner, therefore, pray: Our Father in heaven, Hallowed be Your name. [10] Your kingdom come. Your will be done On earth as *it is* in heaven. [11] Give us this day our daily bread. [12] And forgive us our debts, As we forgive our debtors. [13] And do not lead us into temptation, But deliver us from the evil one. For Yours is the kingdom and the power and the glory forever. Amen. (Matthew 6:9-13 NKJV)

What shall I pray today for your Kingdom to come, Lord?
Am I doing your will Lord?
Is there anything you would like me to pray for your will to be done on earth Lord?
(Man shall not live by bread alone, but by every word that proceeds out of the mouth of God.)
Lord is there anything You would like to say to me today?
Please show me anyone you would like me to forgive and what to forgive them of?
Do I need deliverance from any evil plan or spirit?

When we have finished our daily bread, receiving the specific instructions for the day, we will then pray through our questions for the day based on the pillars.

As we use the answers God gives us, then He will give us more. If we don't use the answers then we will grow dull of hearing. If you don't want to hear the answers, don't ask the questions. You may find some of the questions repeating, as the pillars overlap.

Also remember what we studied in chapter 4 on testing what we hear.

Sunday Pillar 1   Seek first the Kingdom of God

"But *seek first the kingdom of God* and His righteousness.... (Matthew 6:33 NKJV)

This encapsulates all that we are doing for Gods Kingdom and the disciplines that go with that--
Actively building the Church you attend, prayer, Bible study, praise and worship, evangelism, fasting etc..

First pray through the Lord's Prayer.

Questions we can ask on 'seeking first the Kingdom of God'.

Pause after asking each question, ready to write down any response. He may answer, and He may not. He may answer the questions later in the week. But he knows we have asked the questions. Sometimes, I will see the answer, rather than hear it. E.g. when asking who to pray for, I may see their face.
Am I doing enough to build the Church I attend?
What more or less should I do?
Are you happy with my prayer times?
What else should I be doing in my prayer times?
Is there anyone or thing I should be praying for?
Are you happy with my Bible studies?
What should I be studying?
Are you happy with my praise and worship?
What can I do, that would please You?
Are you happy with my evangelism?
What else can I do, or who can I support in it?
Would you like me to fast this week?
If so, when?
Is there any ministry you would like me to help, support, or start?
What else can I do for Your Kingdom Lord?
Dear Holy Spirit, can you suggest any questions I should ask?

Monday Pillar 2   Righteousness/Holiness

> "But seek first the kingdom of God and *His righteousness....* (Matthew 6:33 NKJV)

This is not meant to be a full explanation of the relationship between righteousness and holiness, but simply a few verses to get an overview of the subject.

First of all, as believers, we are the righteousness of God in Christ, it is a gift. This gift is given to us when we make Jesus our Lord, giving our lives to Him.

> For He made Him who knew no sin to be sin for us, *that we might become the righteousness of God in Him.* (2 Corinthians 5:21 NKJV)

> For if by the one man's offense death reigned through the one, much more those who receive abundance of grace and of *the gift of righteousness* will reign in life through the One, Jesus Christ. (Romans 5:17)

But even though we have been given the gift of righteousness it does not mean that our behavior lives up to the standard of the qualities of righteousness.

We have been declared righteous, for the sake of the requirements of the law, by the works of Jesus.
Now we have to learn how to be righteous. Paul tells us to follow righteousness and look to scripture for instruction in righteousness.

> For Christ is the end of the law for righteousness to everyone who believes. (Romans 10:4 NKJV)

Flee also youthful lusts; but *pursue righteousness,* faith, love, peace with those who call on the Lord out of a pure heart. (2 Timothy 2:22 NKJV)

All Scripture *is* given by inspiration of God, and *is* profitable for doctrine, for reproof, for correction, *for instruction in righteousness.* (2 Timothy 3:16)

As we pursue righteousness, and receive instruction in righteousness from the scriptures, we find that there is uncleanness in us. Paul calls this filthiness of the flesh and spirit. As we read the scriptures, we find that it is causing us to be cleansed through washing and as we remove the uncleanness, through confessing our sins, we find that the fruit of righteousness is holiness.

Let us *cleanse ourselves from all filthiness of the flesh and spirit, perfecting holiness* in the fear of God. (2 Corinthians 7:1 NKJ)

Christ also loved the church and gave Himself for her, [26] that He might *sanctify and cleanse her with the washing of water by the word,* [27] that He might present her to Himself a glorious church, not having spot or wrinkle or any such thing, but *that she should be holy* and without blemish. (Ephesians 5:25-27 NKJV)

But now having been *set free from sin,* and having become slaves of God, *you have your fruit to holiness.* (Romans 6:22 NKJV)

Being holy is not a suggestion from our Father in heaven, but a command.

> For God did not call us to uncleanness, but in holiness. (1 Thessalonians 4:7 NKJV)

> Because it is written, "Be holy, for I am holy." (1 Peter 1:16 NKJV)

Not only is it important for us to be holy because God commands us to, we also find that un-confessed sin may be a blockage to healing.

> *Confess your trespasses to one another*, and pray for one another, that you may be healed. (James 5:16 NKJV)

In the book of Hebrews we find that our Father in heaven will chasten us, which is grievous, but that it is so that we may be partakers of His holiness. Then we find out that this holiness is one of the requirements for being able to see the Lord.

> "My son, do not despise the chastening of the LORD, Nor be discouraged when you are rebuked by Him; ⁶ For whom the LORD loves He chastens, And scourges every son whom He receives." ⁷ If you endure chastening, God deals with you as with sons; for what son is there whom a father does not chasten? ⁸ But if you are without chastening, of which all have become partakers, then you are illegitimate and not sons. ⁹ Furthermore, we have had human fathers who corrected *us,* and we paid *them* respect. Shall we not much more readily be in subjection to the Father of spirits and live? ¹⁰ For they indeed for a few days chastened *us* as seemed *best* to them, but He for *our* profit, *that we may be partakers of His holiness.* ¹¹ Now no chastening seems to be joyful for the present, but painful; nevertheless, afterward it yields the peaceable fruit of righteousness to those

who have been trained by it. [12] Therefore strengthen
the hands which hang down, and the feeble knees, [13]
and make straight paths for your feet, so that what
is lame may not be *dislocated,* but rather be healed.
[14] Pursue peace with all people, *and holiness, without
which no one will see the Lord.* (Hebrews 12:5-14
NKJV)

Blessed *are* the pure in heart: for they shall see God.
(Matthew 5:8)

How many ministries have fallen through a lack of holiness?
Working so hard for God they become a target for Satan.
Committed men and women of God can be seduced from the
path of righteousness. We can be most vulnerable when we are
tired, even tiredness from the work of God. Attacks on our
righteousness are not always obvious, they can be subtle. Even
as I am writing this, early in the morning, I had a dream, a
couple of hours ago, where a lady I was praying for in a public
setting, wanted a hug, but then wouldn't let go. In the dream I
thought this was inappropriate and needed to almost push her
away. I then realized as I woke that I had been targeted by a
seducing spirit. The battle will always start in the mind, sin tries
to get into our hearts. This is why we are told to bring every
thought captive to the obedience of Christ.

For the weapons of our warfare *are* not carnal but
mighty in God for pulling down strongholds, [5]
casting down arguments and every high thing that
exalts itself against the knowledge of God, bringing
every thought into captivity to the obedience of
Christ, (2 Corinthians 10:4-5 NKJV)

If we allow ourselves to ponder on thoughts that are unrighteous,
then that thought will grow and then later become sin which

will be worked out in our lives. Jesus put it this way.

> "But I say to you that whoever looks at a woman to lust for her has already committed adultery with her in his heart. **(Matthew 5:28** NKJV)

Jesus was showing us that what goes on in our heart, looking at a woman to lust for her, is the first step to sin.

I do not allow things to happen in my dreams that I would be ashamed of in my normal life.
If anything untoward happens, I take it to Jesus straight away.

Now first pray through the Lord's Prayer.

Questions we can ask on Righteousness/Holiness.

Dear Lord, do I have any un-confessed sin in my heart?
Please show me what the sin is, and give me a sincere repentant heart that I may confess my sin and be cleansed and forgiven.
Is there any other sin I need to repent of?
Have I finished now, Holy Spirit, or is there more to repent of?
Having repented Lord, is there anything you want me to do in response to that repentance?
(E.g. Having stolen, the Lord may want one to return something. Maybe an unkind word to someone, may need a positive one spoken. Etc..)
Dear Lord, are there any thoughts I have had that you consider to be unclean?
Is there anything that I am doing in my life that offends You?
Are there any relationships that I need to be careful with?
Dear Holy Spirit, can you suggest any questions I should ask?

Tuesday Pillar 3   Daily Work/ Your Job

What we do in our daily lives, is vitally important. Not just for the Kingdom of God, but also for our own self-esteem and productivity.

God has created us with different talents, and with a great variety of individual plans for our lives. The work he has for the individual will not always be obviously 'Christian Ministry', but 'individual ministry'. What I mean by that is that the highest callings are not necessarily apostle, prophet, evangelist, pastor and teacher, but maybe school teacher, businessman, sportsman.

Who would have thought that the decision made by the footballer Tim Tebow, to promote 'John 3:16', would impact millions of people. On January 8th 2012 Tebow played his first NFL playoff game, against the Pittsburgh Steelers. He threw for 316 yards, averaged 31.6 yards per completion, the highest single-game postseason completion average in NFL history.

Ben Roethlisberger's second-quarter interception, which led to a Matt Prater field goal and a 17-6 Broncos lead, came on third-and-16, the Steelers finished the game with a time of possession of 31:06. And at the time Tebow threw the game-winning 80-yard touchdown pass to Demaryius Thomas -- the NFL's longest postseason pass in overtime history -- CBS's final quarter-hour overnight ratings were a 31.6.

Millions of people 'googled' the meaning of John 3:16, because of the zeal of this young man to promote God's word. It makes me think how long it would take myself to reach millions of people, as a more traditional minister.

Our highest calling is to fulfill the race that God has set for us individually, whatever that calling may be. The Apostle Paul said that he had completed his race.

> I have fought the good fight, I have finished the race,
> I have kept the faith. (2 Timothy 4:7 NKV)

Now first pray through the Lord's Prayer.

Questions we can ask about our daily work and job.

Father are you happy with me, that I am fulfilling what you have called me for?
Am I doing the specific work/job that you want me to?
Do You want me to change job?
Why do You want me at this job?
Do You want me to take a second job?
Is my daily timetable balanced?
How can I balance my day better?
Dear Holy Spirit, can you suggest any questions I should ask?

Wednesday Pillar 4   Health

Preventative work done in this exercise will save a lot of grief later in life. Many of the problems we experience in life, could have been dealt with before they happened.

> Many *are* the afflictions of the righteous, But the LORD delivers him out of them all. (Psalm 34:19 NKJV)

This promise is wonderful, but wouldn't it be far better to try and avoid some of these afflictions.

Health is a big part of the salvation that Jesus bought for us at the cross.

> To whom has the arm of the LORD been revealed?
> ² For He shall grow up before Him as a tender plant,
> And as a root out of dry ground. He has no form or
> comeliness; And when we see Him, There is no beauty
> that we should desire Him. ³ He is despised and
> rejected by men, A Man of sorrows and acquainted
> with grief. And we hid, as it were, our faces from
> Him; He was despised, and we did not esteem Him.
> ⁴ Surely He has borne our griefs And carried our
> sorrows; Yet we esteemed Him stricken, Smitten by
> God, and afflicted. ⁵ But *He was wounded for our*
> *transgressions, He was bruised for our iniquities; The*
> *chastisement for our peace was upon Him, And by His*
> *stripes we are healed.* (Isaiah 53:1-5 NKJV)

All healing that we receive from God ultimately was paid for at the cross. It was unjust for Jesus to receive the stripes on His back, and therefore He has paid the price for any just, or unjust, reason that we his followers should be afflicted.

There can be many reasons why people are sick, sin is one of them, but is not always the case.
If we have repented, if it was sin, and confessed our faults then we can receive healing.

> Confess your trespasses to one another, and pray for
> one another, that you may be healed. The effective,
> fervent prayer of a righteous man avails much. (James
> 5:16 NKJV)

Healing can also come from other methods:

The laying on of hands.

> They shall take up serpents; and if they drink any

deadly thing, it shall not hurt them; they shall lay hands on the sick, and they shall recover. (Mark 16:18)

And it happened that the father of Publius lay sick of a fever and dysentery. Paul went in to him *and prayed*, and he laid his hands on him and healed him. (Acts 28:8 NKJV)

Anointing with oil.

Is anyone among you sick? Let him call for the elders of the church, and let them pray over him, anointing him with oil in the name of the Lord. 15 And the prayer of faith will save the sick, and the Lord will raise him up. And if he has committed sins, he will be forgiven. (James 5:14-15 NKJV)

Casting out a spirit.

When Jesus saw that the people came running together, He rebuked the unclean spirit, saying to it, "Deaf and dumb spirit, I command you, come out of him and enter him no more!" 26 Then *the spirit* cried out, convulsed him greatly, and came out of him. (Mark 9:25-26 NKJV)

Going to a doctor or hospital.

Yes, this method can work too, in fact the beloved Luke was a physician.

When I'm praying for someone to be healed, I really don't mind what method God chooses to heal them. The important thing for them, is to be healed.

Now first pray through the Lord's Prayer.

Questions we can ask about our health.

Dear Lord, do I have any health issues that I am not aware of?
Do my family and friends have health issues that they are not aware of ?
Dear Lord, am I suffering any affects of un-confessed sin?
Are my family and friends suffering from any affects of un-confessed sin?
Lord, I have been suffering from '.........................' what shall I do about it?
Do you want me to exercise, if so what?
Do you want me to take vitamins or supplements, if so what?
Is there anything else I should be doing to protect my health?
Are there any curses running through my family that can affect our health?
Dear Holy Spirit, can you suggest any questions I should ask?

> *A Psalm* of David. Bless the LORD, O my soul; And all that is within me, *bless* His holy name! ² Bless the LORD, O my soul, And forget not all His benefits: (Psalm 103:1-3 NKJV)

Thursday Pillar 5   Money

This is such an important subject, but is it as important as health, family, holiness, the Kingdom of God? Of course not, but money does matter. I would suggest reading my book or study guide entitled 'MoneyMatters: in My Kingdom.' The Lord asked me to write this book as a 'favor' to Him. It is very comprehensive.

King Solomon of Israel said:

"Money answers everything." (Ecc 10:19 NKJV)

Money is physical, as opposed to spiritual, power.

We need money to pay for all of our personal needs, the upkeep of the Church, and excess to meet the needs of the poor and other Christian projects.

I remember someone saying to me that they only wanted enough money to provide for their needs. They thought they were being humble, but in fact it could be construed as a selfish sentiment. If we only have enough for our own needs, then who is going to help the poor and needy?

Scripture shows us clearly that it is by giving that we receive back and if we give (sow) sparingly, we will reap sparingly, that God is able to make us have an abundance so that we can meet every good work that He wants us to accomplish.

> "Give, and it will be given to you: good measure, pressed down, shaken together, and running over will be put into your bosom. For with the same measure that you use, it will be measured back to you." (Luke 6:38 NKJV)

> He who sows sparingly will also reap sparingly, and he who sows bountifully will also reap bountifully. [7] *So let* each one *give* as he purposes in his heart, not grudgingly or of necessity; for God loves a cheerful giver. [8] And God *is* able to make all grace abound toward you, that you, always having all sufficiency in all *things,* may have an abundance for every good work. (2 Corinthians 9:6-8 NKJV)

Now pray through the Lord's Prayer.

Questions we can ask about our money.

Do I have a pure heart towards money?
Lord is there anything that I should repent of that is blocking me receiving grace?
How do I remove any blockages?
Am I giving enough tithes and offerings to Your church?
Dear Lord, am I earning enough money?
If not—How should I earn more money?
Is there any individual or organization you would like me to give to?
Where should I invest?
Who should be my professional financial consultants?
Am I using the bank, or financial institutes, that You want me to use? If not-- who should I use?
What can I do to leave an inheritance to my children's children?
Dear Holy Spirit, can you suggest any questions I should ask?

Friday Pillar 6   lFamily

Families are very important to God. It is vital that we don't underestimate the time and attention we need to be giving to one another. How many fathers miss their children growing up as they sacrifice time to their work, money and ambition? Absent parents affect the development of the children.

How many ministers of the gospel have time for their flocks and work, yet leave their children deprived? I don't want to be one of them. If I can't love my family, then how sincere is my love for others?

God has called there to be order in the families. The man is the head of the family and has been commanded to love his wife, as Christ loved the Church, giving his life for her. The wife has been asked to submit herself to her husband, as unto the Lord. Children are commanded to obey their parents, with the promise of a blessing for doing so.

> *Wives, submit to your own husbands, as to the Lord.* [23] For *the husband is head of the wife*, as also Christ is head of the church; and He is the Savior of the body. [24] Therefore, just as the church is subject to Christ, so *let* the wives *be* to their own husbands in everything. [25] *Husbands, love your wives, just as Christ also loved the church and gave Himself for her*, [26] that He might sanctify and cleanse her with the washing of water by the word, [27] that He might present her to Himself a glorious church, not having spot or wrinkle or any such thing, but that she should be holy and without blemish. [28] So husbands ought to love their own wives as their own bodies; he who loves his wife loves himself. [29] For no one ever hated his own flesh, but nourishes and cherishes it, just as the Lord *does* the church. [30] For we are members of His body, of His flesh and of His bones. [31] "For this reason a man shall leave his father and mother and be joined to his wife, and the two shall become one flesh." [32] This is a great mystery, but I speak concerning Christ and the church. [33] Nevertheless let each one of you in particular so love his own wife as himself, and let the wife *see* that she respects *her* husband. [NKJ] Ephesians 6:1 *Children, obey your parents in the Lord, for this is right.* [2] *"Honor your father and mother,"* *which is the first commandment with promise:* [3] *"that* it may be well with you and you may live long on the earth." [4] And you, fathers, do not provoke your

children to wrath, but bring them up in the training and admonition of the Lord. (Ephesians 5:22 - 6:4 NKJV)

But if any widow has children or grandchildren, let them first learn to show piety at home and to repay their parents; for this is good and acceptable before God. (1 Timothy 5:4)

Now pray through the Lord's Prayer.

Questions we can ask about our families.

Am I spending enough time with my son, daughter, mother, father, grandmother etc..?
Is there anything I can do to help any member of my family?
Am I training my children properly? If not—what should I be doing?
Am I provoking my children?
Am I submitting and respecting my husband? How should I change?
Am I loving my wife as Jesus loved the Church? How should I change?
Is there anyone that you want me to consider as members of my family? (Spiritual children, brothers, sisters, etc..)
Is there anyone in my family that I should be supporting financially?
Do you want me to adopt an orphan or a widow?
Dear Holy Spirit, can you suggest any questions I should ask?

Saturday Pillar 7   Leisure and Rest

There is sometimes a macho image to excessive work, especially in the business arena, which has no place in the grace of God's Kingdom. If you really want to achieve to the highest of God's abilities you will need to rest, otherwise you may think that it is your work that is bringing about God's plans and works. John the Baptist said 'I must decrease, that He may increase'. That is the same today.

If we plan to be a servant, then we planning to serve the Living God achieve His miracles. No glory for us, because we are 'unworthy servants doing our duty'.

"So you too, when you do all the things which are commanded you, say, 'We are unworthy slaves; we have done *only* that which we ought to have done.'" **(Luke 17:10 NKJV)**

As we read through Luke chapter 17, we find that when the Apostles were asking for their faith to be increased, Jesus addresses the motives of their hearts. Faith was not the problem, the problem was whether we want to receive glory when we do miracles. The right attitude is to acknowledge that the miracles do not come from our own abilities but from God through the obedience of His servants.

Likewise miracle working power can work through our lives if we enter the place of rest. We allow God to work in our lives. Once we start working too hard, we enter a realm where we think we deserve results because of our efforts, rather than allowing Gods work to manifest through us through grace. Grace cannot be worked for.

The Apostle Paul recognized that God's strength was made perfect in his own weakness.

> And He said to me, "My grace is sufficient for you, for My strength is made perfect in weakness." Therefore most gladly I will rather boast in my infirmities, that the power of Christ may rest upon

me. (2 Corinthians 12:9 NKJV)
This is seen in the Old Testament, when Gideon was asked to reduce the size of his army.
And the LORD said to Gideon, "The people who *are* with you *are* too many for Me to give the Midianites into their hands, lest Israel claim glory for itself against Me, saying, 'My own hand has saved me.' (Judges 7:2 NKJV)

Gideons army was reduced from 32,000 down to 300 men. Now with 300 men God was able to give the victory to Israel against an innumerable army of Midianites and Amelekites.

If we want to achieve for God, we must not work for it, we need to enter His rest and allow His works to manifest through us.

"Today, if you will hear His voice, Do not harden your hearts." [8] For if Joshua had given them rest, then He would not afterward have spoken of another day. [9] There remains therefore a rest for the people of God. [10] For he who has entered His rest has himself also ceased from his works as God *did* from His. [11] Let us therefore be diligent to enter that rest, lest anyone fall according to the same example of disobedience. (Hebrews 4:7-11 NKJV)

I use a Hebrew word עוֹלָם `olam, it means 'eternal' in English. When I meditate on this word, it helps me to connect to the eternal part of my spirit.

You see-- in the spirit we are *already sitting in the heavenly places.*

But God, who is rich in mercy, because of His great love with which He loved us, [5] even when we were dead in trespasses, made us alive together with Christ

> (by grace you have been saved), [6] and raised *us* up
> together, and made *us* sit together in the heavenly
> *places* in Christ Jesus, (Ephesians 2:4-6 NKJV)

God wants us to have leisure time. He wants us to enjoy our
lives. Who wants to become a Christian and then be miserable
working all the time? We are not good witnesses to Christ, if we
are working all the time.

My own leisure time is used, watching soccer, going to the
cinema, playing video games with my children, spending time
with my wife in coffee houses. I pray for my soccer team 'Chelsea',
and the Lord blesses them. I even pray for the characters in the
movies I watch. I love bringing Him into my leisure time. I was
once watching a film when one of the characters was put into
jail. I hate injustice and I asked the Lord is He would get him
out, but in a way that I would know it was Him doing it. Well,
in the film a tornado came destroyed the jail and he was released.
An act of God!! How funny when I considered that the Lord
must have had that put it in the script beforehand as He foresaw
me asking Him.
Rick Joyner said that the Lord told him that none of the time
he spent on the golf course would be wasted. We must have rest
and leisure.

What do you do in your leisure time?

Now pray through the Lord's Prayer.

Questions we can ask about our Leisure time and rest.
Dear Lord, can you please show me any areas of my life that I
am striving in?
Lord how do I enter your rest?
Lord am I balanced in my leisure time?
Am I doing anything you disapprove of in my leisure time?

Is there anything you would recommend I do in my leisure time?
Dear Holy Spirit, can you suggest any questions I should ask?

Chapter 21

Conclusion

What do we want to hear when we stand before the throne of God in the Judgment?

'Well done good and faithful servant', is what I want to hear, what I stretch for. I don't want my own personal sufferings to be wasted, to be a life of vanity.

Obedience is better than sacrifice. How can we obey if we don't listen?

> The effective, fervent prayer of a righteous man avails much. 17 Elijah was a man with a nature like ours, and he prayed earnestly that it would not rain; and it did not rain on the land for three years and six months.   (Jam 5:16-17 NKJ)

Like Elijah there is much that can be done through our lives, when we make the choice to be a servant of the Most High God.

This does not mean there will not be failures.

> A righteous man may fall seven times And rise again, (Pro 24:16 NKJ)

I have made some big mistakes, where I have sincerely thought that I had heard, from God, correctly and the outcome has not been what I expected. When learning to walk there are a lot of falls on the way. We must not fear mistakes, but know that we have a loving father who is there to help us when things go wrong. If we fall he will lift us up.

Remember how Jesus reached out for Peter when they were walking on the water, even as Peter was sinking, Jesus was reaching out.

Jesus will help you as you learn to 'Listen to the Voice'.

About the Author

Martin Powell is presently a musician, minister, preacher, teacher, author and businessman. He was born in London, England. His grew up in Nottingham where he studied music—specializing in the clarinet, winning many prizes. Obtaining a music scholarship, he traveled to London to study with Georgina Dobree at the *Royal Academy of Music*, from 1981-1985, and with Guy Deplus, a Professor at the *Paris Conservatoire*, from 1985- 1986. In 1983, he went on to be the first clarinetist to win both the Hawke's clarinet prize and the John Solomon Wind Soloist prize in the same year. Also being awarded the Leslie Martin Scholarship for Clarinet; winner of the Nicholas Blake ensemble Prize; winner of a major award from the Ian Fleming Trust; and finalist in the Haverhill Sinfonia Soloist competition.

He first came to international recognition as a prize winner in the International Clarinet Congress Competition in London in 1984 and winning "Best Musician" in the International Christian Arts for God Competition 2007. He has gone on to perform in England, Germany, Austria, France, Italy, Spain and the USA. He was also the principal clarinet player with the Henry Wood Chamber Orchestra. His clarinet playing has brought him to the attention of many composers. He has given World Premieres of many pieces; both Peter Heron and Wilfred Josephs have written pieces for him. Wilfred Joseph's First and Second sonatas were written for Martin and dedicated to him. The two sonatas were given world premieres at St. John's Smith Square, and the Harrogate International Music festival. Peter's "Soundbites" being premiered at the Purcell Room on the South Bank in September 1996. Other first performances of works by Joseph Horovitz, Mark Andrews, Barton Armstrong, David Llewelyn Green, Christopher Steel and Marjoijn Anstey.

Martin has performed many concertos internationally and at home in the United Kingdom. He has also recorded the music of Debussy, Poulenc, Stravinsky, and many other composers.

As a committed Christian, Martin has dedicated all of his music to God including the many songs the Lord has given to him.

Martin Powell came back to the Lord at the age of twenty-one during the blossoming height of his music career. Being passionate to know God, and being obedient to the calling of the Lord, he sacrificially laid down his clarinet playing in order to know the Lord and to spend time deeply studying the Scriptures, which he has studied intensively for many years.

The Lord then took Martin into business, inspiring him to believe for a three story music store, which the Lord gave him when he was penniless. Now Martin is promoting other Christians in business with the website ChurchTalents.com.

From 1993 to 2010 Martin was the Pastor of the New Haven Fellowship in London. This led to many preaching engagements across the wide spectrum of denominations and independent churches. His preaching has also been transmitted on the Gospel Channel through the Sky Satellite Network.

Out of his study of the Scriptures, the Lord began to give him fresh revelation about the subject of money. In obedience to the Lord, Martin Powell wrote the book 'MoneyMatters in My Kingdom'. God asked him to write it for Him 'as a favor'. It is full of the living Word of God which he prays will be a blessing to you as you apply the principles of this book to your life.

"This is the best book I've ever read on secular or Christian finance." said Rick Joyner, MorningStar Ministries

In 2012 Martin started the business 'Kingdom Talents' manufacturing the Gold and Silver Talents.

To correspond with Martin Powell, please send your letter via email to: Martin@Kingdom-Talents.com. You may also contact us in writing at: Martin Powell, c/o Kingdom Talents, 375 Star Light Drive, Fort Mill, SC 29715.

We would love to hear from you, and welcome your comments. If you desire Martin to come and minister the Word of God and perform his music in your Church, please mention this when you write.

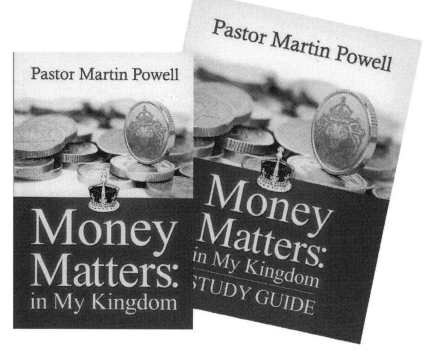